T0278425

Cambridge Elements ≡

Elements in Publishing and Book Culture
edited by
Samantha Rayner
University College London
Leah Tether
University of Bristol

SPACE, PLACE, AND BESTSELLERS

Moving Books

Lisa Fletcher
University of Tasmania

Elizabeth Leane
University of Tasmania

CAMBRIDGE
UNIVERSITY PRESS

Shaftesbury Road, Cambridge CB2 8EA, United Kingdom

One Liberty Plaza, 20th Floor, New York, NY 10006, USA

477 Williamstown Road, Port Melbourne, VIC 3207, Australia

314–321, 3rd Floor, Plot 3, Splendor Forum, Jasola District Centre,
New Delhi – 110025, India

103 Penang Road, #05–06/07, Visioncrest Commercial, Singapore 238467

Cambridge University Press is part of Cambridge University Press & Assessment,
a department of the University of Cambridge.

We share the University's mission to contribute to society through the pursuit of
education, learning and research at the highest international levels of excellence.

www.cambridge.org
Information on this title: www.cambridge.org/9781108738538

DOI: 10.1017/9781108769167

First published 2024

A catalogue record for this publication is available from the British Library.

ISBN 978-1-108-73853-8 Paperback
ISSN 2514-8524 (online)
ISSN 2514-8516 (print)

Space, Place, and Bestsellers

Moving Books

Elements in Publishing and Book Culture

DOI: 10.1017/9781108769167
First published online: May 2024

Lisa Fletcher
University of Tasmania

Elizabeth Leane
University of Tasmania

Author for correspondence: Lisa Fletcher, lisa.fletcher@utas.edu.au

ABSTRACT: From airport bookstores to deckchairs, as audiobooks downloaded by commuters, and on Kindles and other portable devices, twenty-first-century bestsellers move in old and new ways. This Element examines the locations and mobilities of the contemporary bestseller as a multi-format commercial object. It employs paratextual, textual, and site-based analysis of the spatiality of bestsellers and considers the centrality of geography to the commercial promise of these books. *Space, Place, and Bestsellers* provides analysis of the spatial logic of bestseller lists, evidence-rich accounts of the physical and digital retail sites through which bestsellers flow, and new interpretations of how affixing the label 'bestseller' to individual authors and titles generates industrial, social, and textual effects. Through its multi-layered analysis, this Element offers a new model for studying the spatiality of popular fiction.

This Element also has a video abstract: www.cambridge.org/fletcher-leane

KEYWORDS: bestseller, spatiality, novels, marketing, Jack Reacher

ISBNs: 9781108738538 (PB), 9781108769167 (OC)
ISSNs: 2514-8524 (online), 2514-8516 (print)

Contents

1 Introduction

Bestselling novels are found everywhere and are always on the move. These are the books we take on holiday and the ones we read to escape from our everyday lives. Available wherever books are sold, bestselling novels are frequently the first titles we encounter when actively shopping for books. They are the titles that we see most when we walk past bookstores or scroll through online book retail sites, or when we encounter advertisements for new releases in underground train stations or airports, or on the devices that so many of us carry everywhere we go. As book buyers and readers, we associate bestsellers with myriad locations and modes of transport – connections that are reinforced by their cover designs and straplines, and by the lists and media hooks that pull readers towards them. We eagerly turn the pages of bestsellers or press play on audiobooks in homes and cafés, on deckchairs and propped up in bed, soaking in the bath and travelling to work, in the car and on long-haul flights. We leave worn copies behind in holiday homes and donate them to charity shops and street libraries, and post 'shelfies' of our collections on social media. Bestsellers beckon us to seclude ourselves in small towns and tropical islands, promise to spirit us away to imagined worlds and parallel universes, and present themselves as road trips and rollercoaster rides. The bestseller is a fundamentally spatial category in and between its industrial, social, and textual operations.

The category of the bestseller exemplifies the book as an object 'in circulation – both in our cultural landscape and imaginations'.[1] Our conceptual framework and methodologies for investigating the fundamental spatiality of bestselling novels build on the 'genre-worlds model'. Developed by Kim Wilkins, Beth Driscoll, and Lisa Fletcher, this model uses a 'literary sociological approach', acknowledging 'the multiple dimensionality of popular genres: as ever-expanding collections of texts; as social complexes that gather around, produce, and value those texts; and as distinctive sets of industrial practices with various national and transnational orientations'.[2] We argue that this quotation holds just as well if we replace 'popular genres' with 'bestsellers',

---

[1] A. Borsuk, *The Book*. (The MIT Press, 2018), p. 12.

[2] K. Wilkins, B. Driscoll and L. Fletcher, *Genre Worlds: Popular Fiction and Twenty-First-Century Book Culture*. (University of Massachusetts Press, 2022), p. 2.

for two reasons. First, bestselling novels almost always participate in one or more popular genres. Second, we found enormous heuristic benefits in imagining the realm of bestsellers as 'three stacked layers that cannot be easily prized apart: the industrial, the social, and the textual'.[3] We are inspired too by how the genre-worlds model seeks to 'keep alive the spatial metaphorics of the term "world" to talk about places where genre books are written, published, and read, especially given the way that technology has enhanced the international aspects of cultural production'.[4]

We see our approach as an extension of, rather than a departure from, the genre-worlds model, because the category 'bestseller' both cuts through the borders of genre worlds and demarcates them. 'Bestseller' is a powerful label in the highly conventionalised logics and practices of book retail that is only more powerful for its imprecision. Our project in this Element is emphatically not a taxonomic one. We had no interest in tussling with our interviewees about the accuracy of their usage of the term 'bestseller' in our conversations or in critiquing the way the word is (or is not) deployed in their bookshops. To the contrary, with our focus on book retail, we decided from the outset that the bestseller is whatever the people in the industry in our small corner of the world say it is. While our curiosity about all types of bestselling books was sparked time and again by our visits to bookshops, in this Element 'bestsellers' refers to bestselling novels.

Some genre authors and books sell in such volume and so widely that their impact reverberates well beyond their genre heartland. We can think of these bestsellers as, to borrow a phrase from David Glover and Scott McCracken's simple definition of popular fiction, 'those books that everyone reads'.[5] The category of the 'bestseller', however, flexes in relation to the context of its application, one of which is genre. Some novels become bestsellers within a specific genre world but remain virtually unknown beyond its borders. Popular fiction is, as Ken Gelder states, 'essentially, genre fiction';[6] it is also,

[3] Ibid. [4] Ibid., p. 58.
[5] D. Glover and S. McCracken, 'Introduction' in Glover and McCracken (eds.), *The Cambridge Companion to Popular Fiction.* (Cambridge University Press, 2012), p. 1.
[6] K. Gelder, *Popular Fiction: The Logics and Practices of a Literary Field.* (Routledge, 2004), p. 1.

as Glover and McCracken explain, 'usually imagined as a league table of bestsellers whose aggregate figures dramatically illustrate an impressive ability to reach across wide social and cultural divisions with remarkable commercial success'.[7] The category of 'bestsellers' can also function in highly localised, curatorial, or idiosyncratic ways, when, for example, a small-town bookstore promotes a 'league table' based on their sales through a newsletter or window display.

Keeping alive spatial metaphors is key to this Element, which explores how twenty-first century bestselling novels are spatialised in their industrial, social, and textual operations. We argue that the fiction industry creates and exploits this spatiality to move new books as quickly and as widely as possible; to manage and sustain the movement of books to consumers now and into the future; and to frame reading bestsellers as an experience that moves people in multiple senses. We find that the bestseller, as a simultaneously conceptual and commercial category, is understood in relation to spatial contexts. Understanding this flexibility – or extensibility – requires researchers to attend simultaneously to very different localities and scales. We therefore take a mixed-methods approach, combining paratextual, interview- and site-based, and textual analytical methods to examine the localities and mobilities of bestselling novels as multi-format commercial and cultural objects.

From bookstores to bedside tables, from Kickstarter campaigns to Audible subscriptions, from paperbacks to Kindles, bestsellers emerge and circulate today in old and new ways. To give a foretaste of our argument, we begin with short accounts of three novels that became bestsellers as we were conducting our research for this Element in 2022. These analytical vignettes lay the groundwork for our sustained case studies. Aware that the category 'twenty-first century bestselling novels' offers an ocean of choice, for these tasters we plunged in and selected three books that reveal different spatial aspects of the category, accepting that this sample reflects our own perspective on the book market (a spatial point in itself).

---

[7] Glover and McCracken, 'Introduction', p. 1.

1.1 'A Good Bookshop is Like an Airport', or Selling Bestsellers: Emily Henry's Book Lovers

In the week beginning 3 July 2022, *Book Lovers* was one of three novels by Emily Henry on the *New York Times* Combined Print and E-Book Fiction bestseller list. It had sat on the list for seven weeks, having held the #1 slot for two weeks before being displaced by Jack Carr's thriller *In the Blood*. Henry's four titles – *Book Lovers, Beach Read* (2020), *People We Meet on Vacation* (2021), and *Happy Place* (2023) – are audaciously self-referential, making explicit the promise of escape from everyday reality that underpins the marketing of popular fiction. By May 2023, Henry's novels had sold over 2.4 million copies and appeared on the *New York Times* bestseller list for a cumulative 145 weeks.[8] Several commentators speculate that pandemic lockdowns created ideal conditions for Henry's getaway 'romcoms' to become bestsellers, noting that *Beach Read* 'arriv[ed] in the hands of readers at the height of the COVID-19 pandemic'.[9] This view is shared by Henry herself, who points to the books' 'vacation vibe' as central to their appeal: 'We [Henry and her editing team] were very intentional in thinking about the books as mini vacations . . . Part of that is just because it works and part of that is because I myself get that huge craving every summer. When it starts getting hot out, I want a book that feels really escapist.'[10] The 'vacation vibe' of these bestsellers comes from the immediate and literal

---

[8] K. Northover, 'Forget the throbbing euphemisms: These romantic leads go to therapy', *The Age* (25 May 2023), www.theage.com.au/culture/books/forget-the-throbbing-euphemisms-these-romantic-leads-go-to-therapy-20230522-p5daac.html.

[9] A. Kaplan, 'It's always vacation in Emily Henry's world', *Today* (27 April 2023), www.today.com/popculture/books/emily-henry-interview-rcna80292.

[10] Ibid. See also: A. P. Davis, 'The women are smart. The men are sincere. And the ending is always happy. Emily Henry cracked the modern romance novel', *Vulture* (29 March 2023), www.vulture.com/article/emily-henry-romance-novel-profile.html; E. Braidwood, 'The love boom: Why romance novels are the biggest they've been for 10 years', *The Guardian* (14 December 2022), www.theguardian.com/books/2022/dec/13/love-boom-romance-novels-biggest-10-years-young-readers.

association of the act of leisure reading with escape from everyday life (summer reading, holiday reading, beach reads, airport fiction are all synonyms for popular fiction) and the figurative mobilities of books that transport readers outside their reality.

Like all of Henry's novels, *Book Lovers* is a romance centred on a holiday. The book's heroine and narrator is Nora Stephens, a New York literary agent who loves books so much that she wears a fragrance called BOOK – a 'cedarwood and amber blend … meant to summon images of sunbathed shelves and worn pages'.[11] The hero is Charlie Goode, a New York editor who has angered Nora by dismissing a romance manuscript by one of her authors, objecting to its small-town setting. This book, *Once in a Lifetime*, becomes a runaway bestseller.[12] *Book Lovers'* central action is triggered by Nora's married sister Libby, who enforces a small-town romance plot on her single sibling, taking Nora on a holiday to Sunshine Falls in North Carolina – the setting of *Once in a Lifetime*, and, as it turns out, Charlie's hometown. When Charlie agrees to edit *Once in a Lifetime*'s follow-up, *Frigid*, a roman-à-clef about a 'cold-blooded, overly ambitious city slicker' based on Nora herself, the two are forced together.[13]

Nora and Charlie are then the 'book lovers' of the punning title – people who love books and who eventually become each other's lovers. The on-trend cartoon-style covers of the various editions are blatantly

---

[11] E. Henry, *Book Lovers*. (Penguin Books, 2022), p. 104. Bookish scents are readily available, with most promising to evoke paper and woodwork and implying the escapist or transportive power of books: e.g., 'Whispers in the Library' in Maison Margiela's Replica range; 'Paperback' from the Demeter Fragrance Library; 'Book' from Commodity; and Byredo's 'Bibliotèque'.

[12] 'Runaway bestseller' comes into usage in the early twentieth century as a descriptor for a hugely successful book that reaches every corner of a market. Originating in advertised sales to clear very large volumes of stock very quickly, it enhances the intersecting connotations of urgency and newsworthiness at play in contemporary usages of 'bestseller'. 'Must-reads' works in a similar way but stretches to apply to classics, literary fiction, and 'worstsellers'. 'Runaway', *Oxford English Dictionary*, https://doi.org/10.1093/OED/1133568863.

[13] E. Henry, *Book Lovers*, p. 95.

interpellative, summoning passionate readers who want to affirm their love of books. The US Berkley edition shows Nora and Charlie with their backs to each other, each deep in a book while perched on a suitcase overflowing with books. They are back-to-back on the UK/Commonwealth Penguin edition too, each in a rowboat, with the tagline 'One summer. Two rivals. A plot twist they didn't see coming'. The productive tensions between uniqueness and ubiquity, and intimacy and mass sociality in reading a bestseller are also captured humorously in the title of the runaway bestseller, *Once in a Lifetime*.

Book Lovers combines ideas about place, popular genres, and contemporary book retail in ways that speak directly to our interests in this Element. The novel mocks the pleasures of genre fiction and the specific tropes of small-town romance, while affectionately serving them up to readers. Like Henry's other books, *Book Lovers* demonstrates that the metafictional use – parody even – of the spatial clichés of romance and of popular fiction more broadly does nothing to diminish the power of these conventions for readers. Readers expect characters in bestselling novels to be in and move through specific types of places and spaces and are self-conscious enough about this expectation to be unbothered – in fact, entertained – when the generic construction of these sites is made overt. Further, understood as alternative ways of escaping from life's ordinary stresses, leisured travel and reading are equated in the marketing of *Book Lovers* and in the text: 'Maybe this is why people take trips', reflects Nora, 'for that feeling of your real life liquefying around you, like nothing you do will tug on any other strand of your carefully built world. It's a feeling not unlike reading a really good book: all-consuming, worry obliterating.'[14] Bestselling titles themselves are a shorthand for escape: on the plane to Sunshine Falls, Libby, pregnant and mother to two small children, tells Nora that she is 'like three sleepless nights away from snapping and pulling a *Where'd You Go, Bernadette*, if not the full *Gone Girl*.'[15] Henry's brand as a bestselling author embraces and exploits the idea of novels as vehicles for imaginary escape, a marketing tactic that is evident in title choice, cover design, and blurbs. Most pertinent to lay the groundwork for our analysis,

[14] Ibid., p. 171. [15] Ibid., p. 23.

though, is *Book Lovers'* focus on places where books are *sold*. The 'book lovers' of the novel's title corresponds not just to the romantic couple but also to the sisters, who as children lived above a charming independent bookshop in New York called Freeman Books (the name of the store reinforces the novel's gleeful equation of reading with escape). With the young girls' single mother struggling to advance her career as an actor, the bookshop effectively acts *in loco parentis* for them, a place where they while away time reading and then writing shelf talkers signed 'Book Lovers Recommend'.[16]

The title of this international bestseller is thus revealed as a reference to the localised marketing techniques of the fictional bookshop (techniques that we observed in many of the bookshops we studied for this Element). Much of the novel's action happens in Goode Books, an eccentric bookshop in Sunshine Falls owned by Charlie's parents. Despite having fallen on hard times, the shop still emanates 'that warm cedar-and-sunned-paper smell' that so appeals to Nora.[17] Here, she and Charlie work together on *Frigid*, while Charlie looks after the shop for his injured father, and Libby – remembering that small-town romances always feature a subplot about saving a failing business – gives the shop, with its chaotically organised shelves, 'the world's most depressing "café"' and 'lackluster window display', a makeover in the hope that this will stimulate sales.[18] Nora and Charlie consummate their relationship in a bookshop; they decide to move in together in a bookshop; they get engaged in a bookshop.

For Charlie, bookshops have the same transporting effect as books themselves: 'A good bookstore ... is like an airport where you don't have to take your shoes off.'[19] For Nora, bookshops represent happy childhood memories and a sense of home. At one point, she likens her beloved New York to a 'giant bookstore: all these trillions of paths and possibilities'.[20] At the same time, Goode Books, with its down-at-heel dustiness and lack of customers, demonstrates the local impact of changes in the book market. 'It's expensive to keep shops like this up', Nora says, reflecting silently to herself, 'Especially when so many people are turning to

---

[16] Ibid., p. 156. [17] Ibid., p. 117. [18] Ibid., p. 117, p. 68. [19] Ibid., p. 156. [20] Ibid., pp. 225–26.

Amazon and other places that can afford to sell at a massive markdown.'[21] 'Other places' might be taken to be the chains, superstores, and big box stores whose homogeneity and lack of local character directly contrasts the cosiness of Freeman Books and the whimsicality of Goode Books.

These mass-market virtual and physical spaces are almost certainly the same that sent *Book Lovers* to the number one bestseller slot. Henry herself is very active on social media, and her novel, as a page-turning romance, is exactly the kind of book most likely to be sold via Kindle.[22] The invoice for our Kindle copy identifies the 'Item Purchased' as *Book Lovers: The new enemies-to-lovers romcom from Sunday Times bestselling Tik-Tok sensation Emily Henry*. A fragrance based on such an ebook would be a long way from warm cedarwood. While *Book Lovers* relies for its comedy on the knowingness of the bestseller reader when it comes to spatial clichés, it simultaneously romanticises (very literally) the spaces of book retail in ways that belie the nature of its own success. In a world of algorithms and electronic sales, bricks-and-mortar bookshops hold strong cultural significance as embodiments of 'the local' in the book market, a view that we heard strongly echoed in our interviews with booksellers.[23]

1.2 'The Heady Wood-Dust Smell of Freshly Printed Books', or Bookishness and Bestsellerness: R. F. Kuang's Babel

We selected R. F. Kuang's *Babel, or the Necessity of Violence: An Arcane History of the Oxford Translators' Revolution* for our second vignette for two reasons. Both reasons speak to how bestsellers move in more-or-less predictable ways that might feel personal for each book buyer but are utterly conventional (what we might call the *Once in a Lifetime* tension). First, people around us – friends and family – were reading the novel and fully expected that we had read it or added it to our TBR stacks because 'everyone is reading *Babel*'. Second, *Babel's* status as a *New York Times*

[21] Ibid., p. 124.

[22] J. B. Thompson, *Book Wars: The Digital Revolution in Publishing*. (Polity, 2021), p. 37.

[23] For analysis of bookstores as 'meaningful locations' in fiction, see E. J. Muse, *Fantasies of the Bookstore*. (Cambridge University Press, 2022).

bestseller – which evokes images of endless stacks of books – is mirrored in the novel's fixation on the intellectual and sensual pleasures of books and reading (which includes their woody, papery perfume). *Babel*, too, might have been called *Book Lovers*.

Kuang's novel sits at the crossing-place between popular genre fiction and literary fiction. Multiple threads in the novel's paratext tie it to the institutions of high literature, including the subtitle, the dark academia aesthetic of the cover design, the author's note to readers, her bio, and the narrative itself. Kuang's Amazon profile captures the crossover:

> Rebecca F. Kuang is the #1 New York Times bestselling and Hugo, Nebula, Locus, and World Fantasy Award nominated author of *Babel*, the Poppy War trilogy, and the forthcoming *Yellowface*. She is a Marshall Scholar, translator, and has an MPhil in Chinese Studies from Cambridge and an MSc in Contemporary Chinese Studies from Oxford. She is now pursuing a PhD in East Asian Languages and Literatures at Yale.[24]

HarperCollins promoted the book as a 'thematic response' to Donna Tartt's *The Secret History* and 'a tonal retort' to Susanna Clarke's *Jonathan Strange & Mr Norrell*.[25] The novel bristles with references to the nineteenth-century canon.

The thumbnail of *Babel*'s cover on the *New York Times* Print and E-Book list at #15 for 15 January 2023 showed a design for the US edition, like several other titles on the list that week, from both ends of the popular-literary spectrum. The spatial iconography of *Babel's* cover situates it in a web of cultural and social associations that guide consumer choice in conscious and unconscious ways. Directly above *Babel* was Stephen King's *Fairy Tale* (on the list for seventeen weeks and heading down). Both covers feature gold, all-caps, serif font for the author's name and the title, and on

[24] R. F. Kuang, *Amazon Australia* (29 September 2023), www.amazon.com.au/R-F-Kuang/e/B0788VXRHP/ref=aufs_dp_mata_dsk.

[25] 'Babel', *Title Key* (29 September 2023), https://e.hc.com/book/9780063021440.

both covers, the text frames images that promise a fantastic-historical European setting. *Fairy Tale* gives a bird's-eye view of a tower or a tunnel, a brick staircase spiralling into the centre of the book. *Babel*, unsurprisingly, depicts a tower, with the eye drawn across city rooftops in the fore- and midground by birds spiralling up and around it. The immersive verticality and depth of both covers – a visual invitation to enter the book's world – is echoed by other books on the list, including the spiral pull into blue water on Colleen Hoover's *It Starts with Us*, the columnar title and author text over a vertical slice of Hokusai's *The Great Wave off Kanagawa* on Gabrielle Zevin's *Tomorrow, and Tomorrow, and Tomorrow*, and the illustrated frame of Barbara Kingsolver's Appalachian-set *Demon Copperhead*.

This invitation to imaginatively enter a storyworld is intensified in the opening pages of *Babel* by an illustrated map of the City of Oxford, a cross-section of the Babel building, and the 'Author's Note on Her Representation of Historical England and of the University of Oxford in Particular'. The novel's protagonist, born in Canton, takes his English name – Robin Swift – from a child's rhyming book ('Who killed Cock Robin?') and the author of *Gulliver's Travels*. Robin's guardian – Professor Richard Lovell – takes him from Canton to England after the death of Robin's family in a cholera outbreak. *Babel* is a fantastical history of the British Empire in the nineteenth century. The novel's eponymous Oxford college is the heart of the Royal Institute of Translation, where Robin is destined to become a student, and the engine room of the magical technology that powers the Empire, silver-working. The opening chapters establish Robin as the surrogate for the book-loving reader in the text. The only possessions that he 'can't leave behind'[26] in Canton are his books and when he first enters the Professor's study he is 'overwhelmed by the musky, inky, scent of books . . . stacks and stacks of them'.[27] The Professor tells him that Oxford is the 'loveliest place on earth': 'Imagine building after building filled with more books than you've seen in your entire life.'[28] Hiding in plain view here is a visual cliché

[26] R. F. Kuang, *Babel or the Necessity of Violence: An Arcane History of the Oxford Translators' Revolution*. (Harper Voyager, 2022), p. 4.

[27] Ibid., p. 6.   [28] Ibid., p. 23.

(stacks of books) with two main uses in popular culture and abundant on bookish social media: to communicate the joy and wonder of owning and reading books, and to evoke the plenitude of books that need to be stocked, distributed, and sold to create a bestseller.

Babel is utterly a product of the digital literary sphere, at the same time as communicating a yearning for pre-digital book culture. *Babel* was a '#BookTok sensation', 'one of the most anticipated releases' of 2022 in what *The Guardian* calls the 'reading corner of TikTok'.[29] The publisher-coined #enterbabel has attracted thirteen million views worldwide, reinforcing the cover's invitation to readers to enter the novel's world and highlighting the immediate legibility of the textual and visual metaphorics of ingress and travel beloved of publishers.[30] BookTok works in service of print book retail for major publishers, with the hashtags #emilyhenrybooklovers and #enterbabel calling up numerous videos of the various paperback editions: readers' hands fan pages, lift the cover to their face for a kiss, slide it from a bookstore shelf, place it on lovingly arranged bookshelves, or hold it up to the camera with the cover text 'I READ BABEL' or 'What does it feel like to be reading the book you've anticipated for ages?' A scroll through the thumbnails of both # searches reveals immediately the extent to which BookTok acts as a space that both creates and responds to bestsellers, affirming the idea that novels themselves offer imagined spaces for communities of readers to visit and inhabit. These kinds of spaces can be understood as 'affinity spaces', 'sites (which may be abstract rather than concrete) where people come together through shared interests'.[31] Engaging with a bestseller activates simultaneously

[29] R. Touma, 'Babel: The BookTok sensation that melds dark academia with a post-colonial critique', *The Guardian* (8 September 2022), www.theguardian .com/books/2022/sep/08/babel-the-booktok-sensation-that-melds-dark-acade mia-with-a-post-colonial-critique.

[30] #enterbabel, TikTok Creative Center (27 September 2023), https://ads.tiktok .com/business/creativecenter/hashtag/enterbabel/pc/en? countryCode=AU&period=7.

[31] J. P. Gee, 'Semiotic social spaces and affinity spaces' in D. Barton and K. Tusting (eds.), *Beyond Communities of Practice: Language, Power and Social Context.* (Cambridge: Cambridge University Press, 2005), pp. 225–29; Wilkins, Driscoll and Fletcher, *Genre Worlds*, p. 100.

Industrial

Social

Textual

Figure 1 Model of a genre world.[32]

the three layers of the 'Genre Worlds Macaron' described by Wilkins, Driscoll, and Fletcher (Figure 1). As text, commercial product, and social connector, *Babel* – like *Book Lovers* – is saturated by spatial ideas and practices. Our hypothesis, when designing this project, was that the bestseller hyperbolises the spatial logics of the novel as a triply textual, commercial and social phenomenon, not least through the idea of popular narratives as escapist.

1.3 'Stranger in a Strange Land', or All Roads Lead to Amazon: *Shirtaloon's* He Who Fights with Monsters

The self-published fantasy series *He Who Fights with Monsters* by Shirtaloon (aka Travis Deverell) provides a thoroughly twenty-first-century example of an author achieving the classification 'bestseller'. Shirtaloon writes LitRPG or GameLit,[33] a genre in which 'video-game elements appear directly within the story and can be interacted with by the characters'.[34] He identifies the series more broadly as 'portal fantasy'. The series begins

---

[32] Wilkins, Driscoll and Fletcher, *Genre Worlds*, p. 3.

[33] For more about the rise of microgenres such as LitRPG, see: B. Driscoll, 'The rise of the microgenre', *The University of Melbourne: Pursuit* (13 May 2019), https://pursuit.unimelb.edu.au/articles/the-rise-of-the-microgenre.

[34] P. Semel, 'Exclusive interview: "He Who Fights with Monsters: Book Two" author Shirtaloon' (15 July 2021), https://paulsemel.com/exclusive-interview-he-who-fights-with-monsters-book-two-author-shirtaloon/.

when Australian Jason Asano wakes up naked in a hedge maze. The last thing he remembers is 'Playing video games until he got tired and fumbling his way into bed', and he asks aloud, 'What the bloody hell is going on?'[35] A floating screen appears and answers Jason's question: '*You have awoken in a place you do not know. Explore the area to discover more.*'[36] The metaphorics of escape on which the series and its genre depends are especially dense, uniting his characters, video game players, LitRPG readers, and the fans who enter social spaces online in the action of going through a portal to an elsewhere. *He Who Fights with Monsters* literalises the spatial logics of transmedia storyworlds, which perpetuate and amplify the idea – at once industrial, social, and textual in its implications – that consuming narrative is transportive.[37]

Shirtaloon, like other authors of this tightly defined subgenre, generates his income by navigating and fully inhabiting the digital affinity spaces of a specific and highly participatory fandom that delights in tales of escapism. His ongoing success is powered by a digitised and globalised fiction industry that intersects with, but is not dependent on, the infrastructure, personnel, and capital of traditional publishing. Shirtaloon epitomises the successful entrepreneurial author who has found a large and dedicated audience through digital self-publishing across free and user-pays platforms

---

[35] Shirtaloon, 'He Who Fights with Monsters: Chapter 1: Strange business', *Royal Road*, www.royalroad.com/fiction/26294/he-who-fights-with-monsters/chapter/386590/chapter-1-strange-business.

[36] Ibid.

[37] Neither of us had read LitRPG before beginning this Element, but we should share that we are present in a very small way in the series' backstory. Shirtaloon is a University of Tasmania Bachelor of Arts graduate, with a major in English. His Amazon author bio states: 'Shirtaloon was working on a very boring academic paper when he realised that writing about an inter-dimensional kung fu wizard would be way more fun.' Lisa is almost certain she taught the class for which Shirtaloon was writing the 'boring academic paper'. The University's Alumni newsletter reported that the series is an Amazon bestseller, earning Shirtaloon $200,000 a month from subscriptions and sales. 'Humanities showcase: Celebrating a string of successes', *University of Tasmania: News and Stories* (8 June 2022), www.utas.edu.au/?a=1593645.

and by engaging authentically with the social media most relevant to his readers. The inseparability of the layers of the genre-worlds model is strongly evident here. The 'three stacked layers' of the industrial, social, and textual cannot be separated without cross-fertilisation (or cross-contamination, depending on your perspective), an inseparability that characterises the spatiality of bestsellers.

This Element explores the overlap between the mobilities of bestsellers, from the fantasy of imagined escape to the myriad conceptual and physical movements that bring a book to a reader's hands, whether as a trade paperback or a file on an e-reader. This approach highlights the scalar complexity in conceptualising and describing bestsellers – a complexity that has intensified with digitisation and globalisation. The still-growing market for *He Who Fights with Monsters*, a series about 'a modern Australian bloke who wakes up in an alternate reality',[38] suggests the increasing irrelevance of the borders of local and national book markets to genre communities that exist primarily online. Not only is Shirtaloon located far from the traditional centres of publishing, in Tasmania, Australia, but he describes the series' tone as 'modern (and unrepentant) Australian'.[39] Emphatically transmedia and transnational, the series evokes the 'questions of mobilities (between markets, between media forms) that have become more pressing and more complicated in [the twenty-first century] publishing economy'.[40]

This series is a bestseller in the context of the Amazon.com digital publishing ecosystem. You will not find print copies at your local bookshop, including in Shirtaloon's (and our) hometown. For readers new to LitRPG, Shirtaloon recommends Matt Dinniman's Dungeon Crawler Carl series as a read-alike. In October 2022, reporting sales of over 400,000 books across print, ebook, and audio through Amazon, Dinniman signed with global talent agency WME with a view to adapting this series about a 'sadistic game show' for screen.[41] Both Dinniman and Shirtaloon first posted chapters of their stories on the free web

---

[38] P. Semel, 'Exclusive interview'. [39] Ibid.

[40] Wilkins, Driscoll and Fletcher, *Genre Worlds*, p. 58.

[41] A. D'Alessandro, '"Dungeon Crawler Carl" author Matt Dinniman inks with WME', *Deadline* (26 October 2022), https://deadline.com/2022/10/dungeon-crawler-carl-author-matt-dinniman-wme-1235155412/.

novel and fan fiction platform, Royal Road, before finding their way to Amazon. (The Royal Road leads to Amazon: the website identifies itself as an Amazon Affiliate.[42]) After a glowing review was posted on Royal Road's landing page, Shirtaloon's readers increased dramatically, inspiring him to establish a Patreon account to seek revenue. The series evolved quickly from self-published instalments on Royal Road and Patreon to a nine-volume book series available through Amazon Kindle, Kindle Unlimited, Audible, and in paperback. Chapters continue to be published weekly on Shirtaloon's Patreon, with six levels of membership (from Iron Rank at AU$2 a month to Transcendent at AU$80.50 a month in August 2023) offering advanced access to chapters and opportunities to connect with the author and other subscribers through Discord.[43]

Eric Hayot sees in the rapid rise of LitRPG evidence of the fundamental intersections between the forms of the novel and the video game in our 'more general system of narrative media'[44] – an argument that chimes with Wilkins, Driscoll, and Fletcher's analysis of 'transmedia genre worlds'.[45] 'Evaluating genre fiction's role in the transmedia context of publishing', they argue, 'allows us to see and understand the dynamic relationship between the content of books (the textual) and the way they are made public (the industrial)'.[46] Hayot points to Ernest Cline's *Ready Player One* (2011) as the best-known example of LitRPG but explains that the 'vast majority' of texts in the genre 'exist as digital-only objects sold via Amazon's direct publishing platforms'.[47] He sees in LitRPG evidence that the 'field of the novel has been altered by online platforms, and by the kinds of fiction they sell, which tend to be – unlike highbrow fiction – intensely generic and serial'.[48] Typing 'Shirtaloon' into the search field on Literature-Map.com to ask, 'What else do readers of Shirtaloon read?' pops the bonnet on the transnational and transmedia genre engine that Hayot points to. Dinnaman was one of the five closest authors to Shirtaloon on the map on

---

[42] 'The home of web fiction', *Royal Road*, www.royalroad.com/welcome.

[43] 'Shirtaloon', *Patreon*, www.patreon.com/Shirtaloon.

[44] E. Hayot, 'Video games and the novel', *Daedalus*, 150 (2021), 181.

[45] Wilkins, Driscoll and Fletcher, *Genre Worlds*, p. 58. [46] Ibid., p. 75.

[47] Hayot, 'Video games and the novel', p. 181. [48] Ibid.

4 January 2023. The other four – Dakota Krout, Travis Bagwell, James A. Hunter, and Aleron Kong – are all self-published authors of bestselling LitRPG with Patreon- and Amazon-focused business models for multi-format publication. Indeed, eighteen of the forty-six authors on the Shirtaloon map write LitRPG. It makes sense to attach the label of 'bestseller' to individual writers such as Shirtaloon and to his books, whatever their combination of formats, subscription models, or retail venues. Perhaps, though, it would make more sense to consider a collective or aggregate concept of the bestseller, which recognises that the new and evolving logics of the transmedia and transnational fiction industry create thriving chains of consumption for types of stories that completely bypass traditional book retailers. Such an expanded definition would enable, also, a more nuanced analysis of the spatiality of bestsellers as informed by infinitely multiplying real and imagined geographies that are represented, generated, and sustained across multiple media and texts.

1.4 Moving Bestsellers: Key Concepts and Methods

As these three examples show, the bestseller is a fundamentally spatial category, and the dynamics of that spatiality are evolving rapidly in twenty-first-century book culture. Following Rachel Noorda and Stevie Marsden's contention that 'the twenty-first century book requires us to re-examine the very nature and definition of the book in light of its digital forms',[49] we undertook our research with the understanding that print books, ebooks, and audiobooks, and myriad online platforms for selling and buying stories, now exist in parallel. The bestseller is a commercial and cultural category that performs many functions within and beyond the publishing industry, including testing the ever-evolving logistics networks that publishers (including self-publishers) rely on to get books into the hands, or onto the devices, of readers. Bestselling novels move books in the sense that they drive the pace and volume of sales, keeping books flowing along the commercial chain from author to publisher to bookseller to reader and everything in between. Also, whether readers are seeking 'vacation vibes',

---

[49] R. Noorda and S. Marsden, 'Twenty-first century book studies: The state of the discipline', *Book History*, 22 (2019), 373.

a 'helluva ride'[50] or, to '[fall], wholly, happily, into the book',[51] bestselling novels move readers literally and figuratively, as they both circulate as retail products and stir human reactions.

In this Element, we therefore combine two different vantage points to consider the various roles of bestsellers in and as moving books, with a deliberate effort to amplify the spatial pun. We achieve this doubled perspective through two extended case studies, one focused on a specific regional retail book market, the other on a specific book series. Our first case study is a survey-, interview-, and fieldwork-based exploration of a distinctive regional book market – Tasmania, Australia. To deepen understanding of the predictable and not-so-predictable industrial, social, and textual geographies that bestsellers create and sustain, this case study asks what the global book trade in anglophone bestsellers looks and feels like from Australia's southernmost and least populated state. We consider many authors and novels that have been classified as 'bestsellers', but we focus our analysis through our second case study of an indisputable bestseller – Lee Child's Jack Reacher series. We selected this series simply because of that indisputability; other contenders included Nora Roberts and James Patterson. A spatial argument could be made about the work of both authors, but we chose to focus on Child because of the coherence this sustained series provides across publisher, author, genre, and character for a focused Element. The Reacher study uses textual and paratextual analysis, examining the narratives and their commercial packaging (covers, titles, author profiles, straplines, etc.) to consider where bestsellers' function as

---

[50] We are citing here Tracy Wolff's author endorsement for Rebecca Yarros's 2023 bestseller *Fourth Wing* ('Smart-ass. Bad-ass. Kick-ass. One helluva ride!'), but such phrases are standard book marketing parlance. The editorial reviews on the book's Amazon page offer alternatives: 'edge of my seat', 'exhilarating . . . ride', 'buckle up', 'roller coaster ride', 'enjoy the ride'.

[51] An extract from Wendell Steavenson's *New York Times Review* used to promote Nino Haratischvili's historical epic, *The Eighth Life*, marketed as 'The bestselling sensation that UK booksellers are calling this generation's *War and Peace*.' W. Steavenson, 'Who needs a sweeping epic about the red century? You do', *New York Times* (14 April 2020), www.nytimes.com/2020/04/14/books/review/nino-haratischvili-eighth-life.html.

market drivers intersects with their purpose to move readers, in multiple senses.

That bestsellers propel publishing and adjacent industries is amply demonstrated in other volumes in this strand of Elements. In *The Frankfurt Book Fair and Bestseller Business*, Beth Driscoll and Claire Squires argue that bestsellers 'are actively constructed situations in book culture. They are the products of people, practices, sites, materials and events, and they are the instigators of further activity: buying, reading, imitating, avoiding.'[52] Driscoll and Squires's aim is to show the 'workings that produce international bestsellers before the fact'.[53] Our objective, by contrast, is to show the workings that locate and move bestsellers *after the fact*. That is, while thinking about bestsellers inevitably inspires questions about what makes a bestseller (as our interviews with booksellers showed time and again), we hold our focus as much as possible on bestsellers once they are so labelled, without seeking to interrogate the accuracy or currency of the label. In *Writing Bestsellers: Love, Money and Creative Best Practice*, Kim Wilkins and Lisa Bennett answer the question 'What are bestsellers?' pragmatically in relation to the term's historical and contemporary usage, justifying their decision to limit their study to writers who have appeared on the *New York Times* bestseller list: 'Global publishing may happen in many corners of the world but, as writers in the medium-size Anglophone market of Australia, we know that for English-language publishing the United States (and New York particularly) is a massive lodestone.'[54] While Wilkins and Bennett restrict their focus to books and authors that have attracted that 'highly recognisable epithet "*New York Times* bestseller"', they acknowledge that there is 'room for scholarship that explore[s] the notion of "bestsellerness" in smaller markets'.[55] We occupy some of that room by adopting a dual scholarly perspective that is both world-embracing

[52] B. Driscoll and C. Squires, *The Frankfurt Book Fair and Bestseller Business*. (Cambridge University Press, 2020), p. 7.

[53] Ibid.

[54] K. Wilkins and L. Bennett, *Writing Bestsellers: Love, Money and Creative Practice*. (Cambridge University Press, 2021), p. 8.

[55] Ibid.

and close-to-home, oriented both to the pole star of the *New York Times* lists and to the often idiosyncratic 'bestseller' displays of independent bookshops, and sensitive to their interrelation.

Moving Books describes and interrogates the spatial logic of lists and other devices that categorise books as bestsellers and provides evidence-rich accounts of the location of bestselling novels in physical and digital retail sites. Pairing a case study of bookselling in one local market (located on the periphery of the periphery) with an author/series-based case study demonstrates the benefits of mixed methods for research on the space and place of books. This dual case-study approach means that our place-based interpretations of how the label 'bestseller' is affixed to individual authors and titles attend to the bestseller wherever it is found and however it moves, with the caveat, of course, that the inestimable vastness of the category makes any study a partial one that is biased by the researchers' vantage point. Choosing Tasmania for our interviews and fieldwork was, initially, a pragmatic solution devised when COVID-19 squashed our plans to build comparative international case studies, including airport bookshops. As we conducted our interviews and fieldwork, however, our trepidation about the enforced localisation of our methodology gave way to gratitude as we realised that staying closer to home helped us to see things about the bestseller that we may have missed had a pandemic not turned our home state into 'Fortress Tasmania'.[56]

Following the genre-worlds model, the fundamental spatiality of bestsellers is best apprehended through an integrated analysis of their textual, industrial, and social dimensions. We achieve this layered approach – endeavouring to always keep the other layers in view as we attend to each – through integrating close and comparative reading

[56] 'Fortress Tasmania' was a common moniker in the media and everyday conversation in Tasmania at the height of the COVID-19 pandemic after the state's government, led by Premier Peter Gutwein, decided to close the border to mainland Australia to reduce infection rates. Tasmania's distinctiveness in Australia was highlighted by the pandemic; until flights to New Zealand resumed in July 2022, there had been no commercial international flights to or from the state in over two decades.

of books as textual and paratextual objects with engaging with the people and professional practices that locate and move these books as objects for sale. Our specific focus is on where and how bestsellers are sold and bought *as* bestsellers, revealing the extent to which this is always a spatial activity.

Section 2 presents the findings of our regional case study. This research fills a gap in obtaining local data that can be compared with findings from studies in other locales and on larger scales.[57] Our findings confirm the status of bestsellers as the fulcrum of book retail and identify three key and overlapping ways in which their leveraging power manifests: independent bookshops locate themselves industrially through the presence or absence of books by global bestselling authors on their shelves; the books that create the social identity of an independent bookshop are the ones that sell most in their store, with 'bestseller' shelves highly localised; and even when bestsellers are relatively absent from a bookshop's shelves, knowledge about bestselling genres, authors, and texts provides an index for people who buy and sell books, wherever they are.

Section 3 explores the spatiality of bestsellers as texts and commercial products through a case study of Lee Child's Jack Reacher series. Methodologically, it seeks new ways to bring together the close analysis of widely read texts with examination of how those texts are presented as bestsellers. It attends to both the textual meanings generated by the series and to marketing contexts and tactics that bring books to readers, finding a zone of overlap between the textual and industrial that we argue is at the heart of the bestsellers.

---

[57] See: B. Driscoll and D. Rehberg Sedo, 'The transnational reception of bestselling books between Canada and Australia', *Global Media and Communication*, 16 (2020), 243–58; L. Nanquette, 'The global circulation of an Iranian bestseller', *Interventions*, 19 (2017), 56–72; K. Trager Bohley, 'The bookstore war on Orchard Road: A study of contemporary sponsors of literacy and ideologies of globalized book retailing in Singapore', *Asian Journal of Communication*, 20 (2010), 104–23.

Section 4 draws together the elements of our central argument that the bestseller is a fundamentally spatial category. It contends that bestsellers unite in a heightened way the overlapping textual, industrial, and social dimensions of twenty-first-century book culture. To illustrate this overlap, this section examines three devices that guide readers towards bestsellers: bestseller lists; cover straplines that tout books as bestsellers; and 'shelf talkers' in bricks-and-mortar bookshops.

While our approaches and analyses are inevitably informed by our disciplinary position within literary studies, this Element fits squarely within twenty-first-century book studies as it is described by Noorda and Marsden. Responding to Simone Murray's 2006 mapping of the field, Noorda and Marsden propose three nodes for twenty-first-century book studies, to all of which this Element seeks to contribute: 'digital (con)texts, the economics of the book trade, and the cultural industry and economy'.[58] As English academics, we have tried to be alert also to the need to model research that explores the connections between the 'outside' and the 'inside' of books. This Element enacts our strong commitment to the value of reading novels as a research method to investigate questions across all three of Noorda and Marsden's nodes. It provides a combination of concepts and methods that we hope will be transferable to research on other types of books, or, indeed other retail markets.

2 The Bestseller in the Local Bookshop

As a marketing label 'bestseller' is so ubiquitous and the criteria for its application so variable that it can feel worn out through overuse.[59] As Brigid Magner explains, 'the term "bestseller" is elastic and depends on context for its significance'.[60] Our interest is therefore not to seek definitional precision, but to focus on the everywhere-ness of bestsellers. We are

---

[58] Noorda and Marsden, 'Twenty-first century book studies', 381; S. Murray, 'Publishing studies: Critically mapping research in search of a discipline', *Publishing Research Quarterly*, 22 (2006), 3–25.

[59] B. Magner, '*Shantaram*: Portrait of an Australian Bestseller', *Antipodes*, 28 (2014), 220.

[60] Ibid.

guided also by Driscoll and Squires, who propose a theorisation of the 'bestseller as situation'. Bestsellers, they argue, 'are situations that both confirm and disrupt patterns of global book commerce and the scholarship that attends to it'.[61] For this section, we went looking for 'bestsellers' in the region where we live and asked people who sell and buy novels to share their experiences of engaging with books labelled 'bestsellers', however they understand or feel about them. This section asks, how are bestsellers situated for participants in book culture in a specific geographical location?

Australian literary novelist Charlotte Wood, in her article 'Reading isn't Shopping', laments the 'explosion of consumer culture' and its influence on literature.[62] Horrified by publisher tactics 'in the pursuit of higher sales' – for example, money-back guarantees, book-club questions in the back matter – Wood is disturbed by the 'incursion of these marketing tendrils into the pages of the book itself'. Contrary to Wood, we are not offended by a 'connection between consumerism and reading' but find in bestsellers a powerful reminder that *reading is shopping*. To consider how bestsellers create and sustain this truth as always already textually, industrially, and socially situated (even for those who, like Wood, find it 'dangerous'), we use a mixed-methods approach, drawing on survey data, interviews, and site-based observation to consider the place of bestsellers in the local bookshop.

We opened this Element by contending that bestsellers are found everywhere and are always on the move, a claim that conceptualises the category as extensible, hyper-visible, and reaching every nook and cranny of commerce and culture. This section narrows down 'everywhere' to a relatively small area, using a specific case study to bring out larger points. Our case study comprises a group of independent bricks-and-mortar bookshops spread across the island state of Tasmania, off the southeast coast of the Australian mainland. Popularly conceived as lying at the end of the inhabited world, with a population of just over half a million, and with 40 per cent of its land area devoted to government-managed parks and

---

[61] Driscoll and Squires, *The Frankfurt Book Fair*, p. 7.

[62] C. Wood, 'Reading isn't shopping', *Sydney Review of Books*, 14 August 2018, https://sydneyreviewofbooks.com/essay/reading-isnt-shopping/.

reserves,[63] Tasmania is a long way – in multiple senses – from the northern hemisphere cities in which bestsellers are often written, published, and set. Our decision to focus on Tasmania was on one level pragmatic: we live there, and our research was planned and conducted during the COVID-19 pandemic, when we were unsure what travel would be possible. However, as we COVID-proofed our project design, we were increasingly influenced by David Carter's assertion that 'the transnational nature of popular fiction networks is best appreciated from the perspective of one of their more remote nodes, rather than from the largest and most powerful centres from which we habitually take our bearings'.[64] Racking focus from Tasmania to the world and back again for a study of the spatiality of the bestseller convinced us through experience that the view from the periphery (or even, in our case, the periphery of the periphery) *can* be especially illuminating.

Our focus on independent bookshops follows a similar logic. These retail sites are routinely positioned in opposition to the bestseller: their 'modus operandi' argues Gemma O'Brien, is to 'hand-sell small selections in low volumes (small and slow)', even while they operate within a market that 'favours fast, high volume selling'.[65] Laura J. Miller enunciates the tension in independent bookshops' dual orientation towards literature as art and bookselling as commerce in her US-focused study, *Reluctant Capitalists: Bookselling and the Culture of Consumption.* 'Book professionals', she finds, 'habitually deplore the prominence of bestsellers, but at the same time continuously chase after the next blockbuster that can bring them quick riches.'[66] Marketing academic Stephen Brown captures the tension with his

[63] 'Reserve listing', *Tasmania Parks and Wildlife Service*, https://parks.tas.gov.au/about-us/managing-our-parks-and-reserves/reserve-listing.

[64] D. Carter, 'Beyond the Antipodes: Australian popular fiction in transnational networks' in K. Gelder (ed.), *New Directions in Popular Fiction: Genre, Distribution, Reproduction.* (Palgrave Macmillan UK, 2016), p. 349.

[65] G. T. M. O'Brien, 'Small and slow is beautiful: Well-being, "socially connective retail" and the independent bookshop', *Social and Cultural Geography*, 18 (2017), 573–76.

[66] L. J. Miller, *Reluctant Capitalists: Bookselling and the Culture of Consumption.* (Chicago University Press, 2007), p. 85.

playful aphorism 'beanz means books' (another way of saying reading is shopping): 'Books are special, some say, and should be treated as such. Books are the new baked beans, others proclaim, and should be sold as such.'[67] Just as we hope our vantage point on the periphery provides a useful slant on transnational networks, so exploring sites where bestsellers are considered most anomalous or 'dangerous' (to use Wood's anxious descriptor) provides unique insights into how this category flexes across scale, location, and context.

These two factors – remoteness and independent bookshops – are interconnected. In a study of independent bookshops in Sydney, Jen Li found that this sector of the book industry was faring better in Australia than in the US or UK, due to the continent's distance from major online retailers; the relative lack of large shopping centres; and the less aggressive nature of chain bookshops in the country.[68] All of these factors, if true for Sydney, are likely to be even more true for Tasmania and other regional or remote locations. This might explain why, of the twenty-six substantial physical retailers of books in the state that we identified, including discount department stores (DDSs), nearly half were independent bookshops. Another factor, in our case, is that independent bookshops have seen a resurgence since Li published her article in 2010.[69] It is beyond the scope of this Element to conduct economic analysis of the relative size and health of the independent book retail sector in Tasmania, but we are confident that people in the state believe they value local independent bookshops more than 'mainlanders'. When Fullers Bookshop in Hobart, the state's capital, celebrated its centenary in 2020, Tasmanian novelist

---

[67] S. Brown, 'Preface: Beans means books' in S. Brown (ed.), *Consuming Books: The Marketing and Consumption of Literature*. (Routledge, 2006), p. xiii.

[68] J. Li, 'Choosing the right battles: How independent bookshops in Sydney Australia compete with chains and online retailers', *Australian Geographer*, 41 (2010), 260.

[69] See: Z. Wood, 'Indie bookshop numbers hit 10-year high in 2022 defying brutal UK retail year', *The Guardian* (6 January 2023), www.theguardian.com/books/2023/jan/06/indie-bookshop-numbers-hit-10-year-high-in-2022-defying-bru tal-uk-retail-year.

and Fullers bestselling author Danielle Wood remarked, 'Tasmania is the single best place in the world to be either a writer or a reader, because we have such great bookshops and we have such an amazing literary community.'[70]

While others have examined the ways in which bestsellers move across the globe,[71] our interest is rather in what happens once they reach a physical bookshop in a distinctive location. Empirical studies of bookshops have become increasingly common in recent years,[72] and several include spatiality as a focus,[73] but none is specifically interested in how global bestsellers function in these local retail contexts. Our method comprises three parts: an online survey of over one thousand Tasmanians about their novel-buying practices; in-depth interviews with booksellers at seven independent bookshops in five Tasmanian cities and towns; and detailed observation of the spatial layout of these same bookshops.[74] While our data is drawn from Tasmanian bookshops, and the island's place identity – its location, history, demographics, and culture – is important background to our analysis, this section is not concerned with how that identity manifests in bookshops. We are interested instead in the function and influence of bestsellers in the

---

[70] L. MacDonald, 'Fullers Bookshop celebrates 100 years as others fall by the wayside', *ABC News* (16 February 2020), www.abc.net.au/news/2020-02-16/fullers-bookshop-defies-trend-celebrates-100th-birthday/11967110.

[71] See: Driscoll and Rehberg Sedo, 'The transnational reception of bestselling books', 243–58; Nanquette, 'The global circulation of an Iranian bestseller', 56–72.

[72] See: C. Squires, *Marketing Literature: The Making of Contemporary Literature in Britain* (Palgrave Macmillan, 2007), pp. 94–7; K. Trager Bohley, 'The bookstore war on Orchard Road', 104–23; B. Luyt and A. Heok, 'David and Goliath: Tales of independent bookstores in Singapore', *Publishing Research Quarterly*, 31 (2015), 122–31.

[73] See: O'Brien, 'Small and slow is beautiful', 573–95; A. Steiner, 'Select, display, and sell: Curation practices in the bookshop', *Logos*, 28 (2017), 18–31; Li, 'Choosing the right battles', 247–62; A. Laing and J. Royle, 'Examining chain bookstores in the context of "third place"', *International Journal of Retail & Distribution Management*, 41 (2013), 27–44.

[74] M. Giovanardi and A. Lucarelli, 'Sailing through marketing: A critical assessment of spatiality in marketing literature', *Journal of Business Research*, 82 (2018), 149.

spatial relations of bookshops and in how the specific location of the bookshop inflects the concept of the bestseller.

We found that the global bestseller has a key role in local independent bookshops, even when it is conspicuously absent, acknowledging the scope of this study is limited to anglophone bestsellers and thus privileges some parts of the world more than others. But bestsellers do not need to cross borders to be understood as bestsellers: they can also be national, regional, local, and even hyper-local, as when an author or book outsells others in a single bookstore but nowhere else. The category of bestseller, so often thought of as homogenising and flattening, is malleable and adaptable in ways that independent bookshops happily exploit to sell books. Inasmuch as it is legible to booksellers and customers alike, the bestseller is a fundamentally situated textual, industrial, and social category. A key finding of our Tasmanian-based case study is that bestsellers, whether present or absent, drive the book market, even at the ends of the Earth.

2.1 'The Pleasure of the Purchase': A Survey of Novel-Buying Practices

The first part of our empirical research, conducted statewide, provides context for the more detailed and intimate information gleaned from our interviews with booksellers and observations of book retail spaces. We asked over a thousand Tasmanians about their book-buying and related practices through an established survey tool, 'The Tasmania Project' (TTP).[75] Running periodically since April 2020 and administered by the Institute for Social Change at the University of Tasmania, TTP aims to gauge the priorities, needs, and desires of residents of the state. While standard data is gathered in each round of the survey, researchers can add sets of questions on specific issues. Our questions were included in the seventh round of this larger survey (TTP7), which dealt broadly with 'Place and Well-Being' and ran online from 15 June to 7 July 2022. The survey participants comprised 992 respondents drawn from a previously recruited TTP 'panel sample' of 3,831, contacted via email, together with

---

[75] See: 'The Tasmania Project', *University of Tasmania: Community and Partners*, www.utas.edu.au/community-and-partners/the-tasmania-project.

a newer cohort of 306 respondents recruited via social media. All respondents were eighteen years or older and resident in Tasmania. The survey thus had 1,298 responses, 38 of which were partially (over 50 per cent) complete. Of these 1,298 respondents, 224 people indicated that they do not buy novels and were excluded from our section of the survey, leaving 1,074 respondents, although not all of these answered every question of our section. The Tasmania Project collects both quantitative and qualitative data, which provides us with a broad and rich sense of the book-buying motivations and practices of those surveyed.

Unsurprisingly for an opt-in survey, TTP7 results demonstrate a selection bias, with respondents more likely to be female, fifty-five years or older, Hobart-based, and better educated than census statistics would suggest for a non-biased sample. Although normally data would be weighted to better reflect the demographics of Tasmanian residents, in this case, we decided not to do so. In Australia, book readers tend to be 'tertiary educated women aged between 30 and 59', with people aged thirty to fifty-nine years making up nearly half of frequent readers, and those sixty or over comprising nearly two-fifths.[76] Book reading is admittedly not the same as book-buying, and Tasmanian readers may differ demographically from the Australian average. For these reasons, we present our survey data with some caution, while contending that our sample is a good enough demographic fit with the Tasmanian book-buying public to make it useful for our contextual purposes.

We asked respondents three questions:

- What kinds of novels do you mostly buy? This question was multiple choice, with the option of selecting up to three answers, and to add a text-based answer under 'other' if required. Those who indicated here that they did not buy novels were not asked further questions and were excluded from our data.
- Where do you buy the majority of your novels? This question was multiple choice, with one answer allowed, and the ability to give a text response under 'other'.

---

[76] Macquarie University and the Australia Council for the Arts, 'Reading the reader: A survey of Australian reading habits', *Australia Council* (2016), https://australiacouncil.gov.au/advocacy-and-research/reading-the-reader/.

- Why are [the answers to the respondent's second question] where you buy the majority of your novels? This answer was text-based and provided qualitative data that we coded thematically.

Because we are interested in bookshops and book-buying, rather than book-reading practices, in this survey we did not include libraries or other non-commercial options in the third question, although some respondents indicated that this was the only way they accessed novels. Unsurprisingly, bestsellers are among the most frequently borrowed books in Tasmanian libraries. Indeed, in 2022, the most borrowed adult fiction title was Child's *Better Off Dead* (2021). Other genre novels by bestselling national and international authors such as Michael Connelly, Anne Cleeves, Liane Moriarty, and Garry Disher occupy the top ten most-borrowed titles.[77]

The results for the first two (quantitative) questions are given below (Figures 2 and 3). About 30 per cent of responses to the question of what kinds of novels are purchased indicated literary or general fiction (remembering that an individual could enter up to three responses). Crime/thriller was the next largest category of responses (19 per cent), followed by historical fiction (17 per cent) and sci-fi/fantasy/horror (14 per cent). This is the same ranking order as that found in the list of most read fiction genres in a 2016 survey of nearly 3,000 Australians, *Reading the Reader*.[78]

Two-thirds of respondents nominated physical stores as the primary place they buy novels, with the majority of these (62 per cent) – just over 40 per cent of the whole sample – indicating dedicated bookshops located in Tasmania selling new books (i.e., independents and chains) as their most common option. Only 8 per cent of the physical-bookshop-buying cohort (5 per cent of the whole sample) chose to shop primarily at DDSs, and another 27 per cent of this cohort (18 per cent of the whole sample) shopped mainly at second-hand

---

[77] 'Tasmania's Top 10s of 2022', *Libraries Tasmania*, https://libraries.tas.gov.au/news/top10sof2022/.

[78] Macquarie University and the Australia Council for the Arts, 'Reading the reader', pp. 11–12. This survey is nationally representative. Note that it uses three categories – 'Contemporary/general fiction', 'Classics', and 'Literary Fiction' where we use one (Literary/general fiction). Also, respondents were younger than those for TTP7 – fourteen years or older.

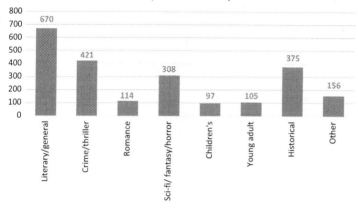

**WHAT KINDS OF NOVELS DO YOU BUY MOSTLY?
(SELECT UP TO 3)**

Figure 2 Answers to our first TTP7 survey question, 'What kinds of novels do you mostly buy?'

stores. A third of the whole sample selected online retailers as the source of most of their purchased novels, with the majority of these (63 per cent) buying ebooks, and 37 per cent buying their books (print and ebooks) from Amazon. These results roughly reflect the book-buying behaviour of Australians more generally reported in *Reading the Reader*, with more Australians purchasing books from bricks-and-mortar stores than online.[79]

Most interesting for our purposes were the answers to the third, text-based question, 'Why is this where you buy the majority of your novels?' We grouped these responses according to the corresponding answer to question two, and then manually and inductively coded them with the help of our research assistant, Caylee Tierney. Our coding framework is outlined in Figure 4.

People who indicated that they bought most of their novels at local bookshops did so first because they found pleasure in the physical and

[79] Ibid., p. 16.

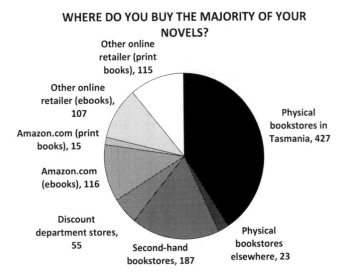

Figure 3 Pie chart indicating the results of TTP7 survey respondents to our second question, 'Where do you buy the majority of your novels?'

material environment of the bookshop (and the physical and material qualities of books themselves);[80] and then, because they valued and wanted to support local community and business. Many appreciated the opportunity to interact with staff and other customers. 'I love the connection with bookstores', wrote one respondent: 'recommendations from staff and writers, talks in the evenings, social connection and seeing the books. Bookstore[s] also smell amazing!!!!'[81] The reference to smell specifically was repeated by four other respondents, with the sensory

---

[80] This category included both independent and chain bookshops, but only two of the thirteen physical bookshops in Tasmania that we identified are chains. Where specific bookshops were mentioned by survey respondents, they were almost always independents.

[81] Written response from The Tasmania Project 7 data.

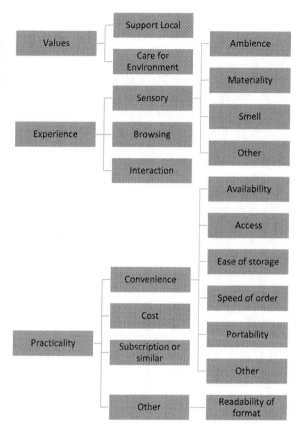

Figure 4 Coding framework for text responses to the third TTP7 survey question.

pleasure of book-shopping highlighted by respondents who choose independent bookshops. Another respondent wrote, 'The pleasure of a book is handling it, discussing the author with the bookshop owner/seller, exploring taste along the shelves – [you] just cannot do this online.'

'Service, keeping jobs locally and when I go in, they know me!!' wrote a third. Local bookstores were positioned by one respondent in direct opposition to DDSs in terms of cost versus curation: 'Big W has cheap books but no specialist knowledge.' Of particular interest to us in terms of spatiality was an emphasis on the ability to browse – something explicitly mentioned (without prompting) in 27 per cent of codable responses from those who buy novels at local bookshops. One respondent termed browsing before buying 'part of the pleasure of the purchase'. Another liked physical stores because they provide something the online environment cannot: '[Y]ou can browse in person, flick through the pages and maybe stumble upon something you wouldn't have if you were using a search engine online.' This emphasis on browsing corresponds with findings from surveys conducted elsewhere.[82]

The motivations for purchasing at venues other than bricks-and-mortar bookshops were more about practicality than pleasure. Those who bought most of their books at DDSs overwhelmingly indicated cost as the key factor in their choice. Those who mostly bought books online (print and ebooks) did so primarily because of practical reasons: first, convenience – availability, access, quick delivery, and ease of storage (in the case of ebooks) – and then cost. A small number of those who purchased ebooks did so because of environmental benefits. The ability to browse virtually was a motivator for only two respondents who purchased mainly online. One of these disliked the 'knocking and jostling' against other people that they believe accompanies this activity in physical stores. As this comment shows, there is no reason why physical browsing cannot have an online equivalent – indeed, the program via which websites are displayed is called a browser, due to its original function of enabling viewers to locate and access documents and files.[83] Nonetheless, our data suggest that the online environment, with its engines and algorithms directing the shopper towards titles that a machine has calculated should

[82] See Laing and Royle, 'Examining chain bookstores', who focus on chain bookshops, particularly pp. 33–34.

[83] 'Browser', *Oxford English Dictionary*, https://doi.org/10.1093/OED/8779534421; 'Web: Web browser', *Oxford English Dictionary*, https://doi.org/10.1093/OED/9315729594.

interest them most, is perceived by the respondents in direct opposition to bookshop browsing.

Several critics have spelled out in detail the way in which local – and especially independent – bookshops are characterised in the book market: as personalised, community-focused, distinctive alternatives to what is considered the homogenising, impersonal, commercially driven nature of large-scale (particularly online) retailers.[84] In terms of book buyers' motivations for shopping at bricks-and-mortar independent stores, then, Tasmanians are typical of book buyers more generally. However, some surprising results become evident when the unit of analysis moves from the meso-space of the whole state to the micro-space of the individual bookshop.

2.2 Booksellers and Bestsellers: Site-Based Interviews and Observations

According to a popular piece on 'the most bookish cities in the world', Lisbon, Portugal, has the highest number of bookstores per 100,000 people (approximately 42), although Melbourne, Australia, is runner-up at about 34 per 100,000.[85] On this scale, Tasmania – 400 kilometres south across the shallow, rough Bass Strait from Melbourne – does not rank highly. By our count, the island, which has a population of around 570,000,[86] has only 13 dedicated bookshops scattered through its cities and towns (see Figure 5) – just over 2 per 100,000. This is perhaps not surprising, given the cost of books and the demographics of Tasmania compared to national figures: the island has 'the highest proportion of people living in disadvantaged areas', the 'poorest level of educational attainment' and the lowest income levels of any state or territory in Australia.[87] Given the typical demographics of DDS

---

[84] See: Miller, *Reluctant Capitalists*; O'Brien, 'Small and slow is beautiful'; Li, 'Choosing the right battles'.

[85] A. M. Y. Jansen, 'The most bookish cities in the world', *Book Riot* (2 July 2021), https://bookriot.com/bookish-cities/.

[86] 'National, state and territory population', *Department of Treasury and Finance Tasmania*, www.treasury.tas.gov.au/Documents/Population.pdf.

[87] 'Drivers of Tasmania's future population health needs', *Department of Health (Tasmania)* (June 2020), www.health.tas.gov.au/sites/default/files/2022-06/

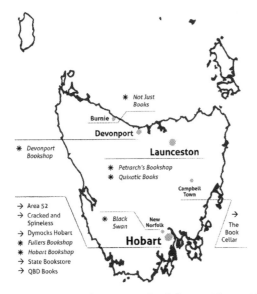

Figure 5 Map of Tasmanian bookshops, with asterisks marking those where we conducted interviews and fieldwork, and arrows indicating the remainder.

book-buying,[88] it may appear surprising that of Tasmania's thirteen book-shops, eleven are independent. However, due to Tasmania's small and dispersed population and the logistical challenge of freight to an island, unlike the mainland states it has not attracted many of the international big-box chains (e.g., IKEA, Aldi, UNIQLO, Costco), limiting the retail economy. Over half of the bookshops are based in the capital, Hobart, although only

Drivers%20of%20Tasmania%27s%20Future%20Population%20Health%20Needs_0.pdf.

[88] Miller, *Reluctant Capitalists*, p. 95 observes that 'Mass merchandisers, super-markets, drugstores, and mail-order book clubs still cater to a greater percentage of lower-income and lower-education readers than do chain or independent bookstores'.

a third of the state's population lives in that city.[89] The two chains are both Australian; both claim a history stretching back to the nineteenth century; and both have multiple stores throughout the country (as well, in Dymocks's case, as in Singapore and New Zealand).[90] Unsurprisingly, international chains, such as Dillons, Barnes and Noble, and Kinokuniya, have an Australian but not a Tasmanian presence. Additionally, we identified thirteen DDSs (including Kmart, Target, and Big W) in the state that sell books.

Of the thirteen Tasmanian bookshops we identified and approached, we were able to undertake interview- and site-based research at seven, all of them independent. As context for our findings, we provide here a summary of the location, self-characterisation, and (where relevant) specialities of these bookshops.

In the south of the state, our sites were The Hobart Bookshop and Fullers Bookshop in the capital city and Black Swan Bookshop in the nearby town of New Norfolk (population just over 6,000). First opened in 1990 and changing hands in 2020, The Hobart Bookshop is in an early nineteenth-century sandstone warehouse in Salamanca Square, the hub of Hobart's historical and tourist district. Unsurprisingly, given this location, the shop boasts 'a huge Tasmanian section', although it also offers 'the largest range of children's books in Tasmania. Probably', as well as a small selection of second-hand titles.[91] Its primary competitor, Fullers, is located in the Central Business District (CBD), in what in the UK might be termed the 'high street' – undeterred by the presence nearby of one of the chains, Dymocks.[92] In the context of our seven sites, Fullers Bookshop is large in

---

[89] 'Snapshot of Tasmania: High level data summary for Tasmania in 2021', *Australian Bureau of Statistics* (28 June 2022), www.abs.gov.au/articles/snapshot-tas-2021. This population figure refers to Greater Hobart.

[90] 'About QBD', *QBD*, www.qbd.com.au/site/about/; 'About', *Dymocks Books and Gifts*, www.dymocks.com.au/about.

[91] 'Salamanca's independent bookshop', *The Hobart Bookshop*, www.hobartbookshop.com.au/page/about.

[92] This positioning reinforces Li's statement that independent bookshops tend to be in the high street, and chains in shopping centres, although not her observation that in Australia, the two tend to be a long way apart spatially, and hence not in close competition ('Choosing the right battles', p. 255). This may be because Li's

terms of floor space and has a sizeable café. The bookshop strongly promotes its long history in the state: 'Masterful recommenders, curious readers, eccentrically knowledgeable, community proud – since 1920'.[93] About a forty-minute drive north along the river Derwent, Black Swan Bookshop is much smaller, with a tiny café, catering to a more niche customer base; for instance, part of their collection appeals specifically to architecture buffs. A block or two away from New Norfolk's main street, the shop attracts about a fifth of its custom from interstate and international tourists, with the remainder split between locals and Hobartians who consider the travel time a worthwhile investment.[94]

The remaining four bookshops are in the state's north, in the next three largest cities after Hobart. In Launceston (population around 67,000), we undertook fieldwork at Petrarch's Bookshop and Quixotic Books, both on the same street in the CBD. Housed on the first floor of a colonial building, and having opened only a year before we visited, Quixotic Books specialises in 'difficult to find' titles and has especially strong holdings in historical fiction.[95] Just ten houseblocks away in a modern street-level premise is Petrarch's Bookshop, a Launceston fixture since 1985, which happily offers 'bestselling titles' while putting a special emphasis on 'Tasmaniania'.[96] In Devonport (population 26,000), we visited Devonport Bookshop, a long, narrow venue in the CBD, sporting a book-themed mural on an outside wall (Figure 6). The shop has 'provided a haven for readers' in the region for nearly thirty years, offering a 'friendly, relaxed space with a carefully chosen range of books'.[97] Our last site is Not Just Books, in the centre of the

❧

study occurred in Australia's largest city (Sydney), whereas Tasmania's CBDs are much smaller.

[93] 'About Fullers Bookshop', *Fullers Bookshop*, www.fullersbookshop.com.au/.

[94] Alexander Okenyo (Black Swan Bookshop), personal interview (21 October 2022).

[95] 'Quixotic Books', www.quixoticbooks.com.au/; Toby Wools-Cobb (Quixotic Books), personal interview (28 November 2022).

[96] 'About us', *Petrarch's Bookshop*, www.petrarchs.com.au/about-us.

[97] 'About', *Devonport Bookshop*, www.devonportbookshop.com.au/pages/4693-ABOUT.

Figure 6 A book-themed mural on the back wall of Devonport Bookshop.

small city of Burnie (population just under 20,000). Around thirty years old and family-owned, the shop sells a wide variety of items including station-ery, gifts, games, and toys plus, on their own assessment, an 'enormous range of fiction'.[98] All the shops have websites that enable customers to purchase their titles online. As this introduction indicates, there is consider-able diversity in terms of purpose, brand, and customer-base even within this small group of independent bookshops.

---

[98] 'About us', *Not Just Books*, https://notjustbooks.com.au/pages/about-us.

Our interviews with booksellers (owner-managers and managers) were
semi-structured, focused around three key questions (provided to interviewees
in advance) addressing the place of the bestseller in the bookshop in question;
the factors influencing the display of bestsellers in the shop; and – as a link to our
global case study – whether the Reacher series is a bestseller in their shop. Our
interview technique was influenced by Danielle Fuller's approach to her interviews with writing communities. Fuller explains that 'by deferring to the
interviewee's experience and knowledge, I was able to demonstrate my respect
for [the interviewee] and to convey my own awareness that I was an outsider
who had to earn the trust of the communities' under investigation.[99] As industry
outsiders, we likewise approached interviewees as sources of experience and
knowledge. Our interviews were complemented by detailed observation and
recording through photographs of the spatial layout of the store, including the
outside of the premises and window displays, following a series of guiding
questions prepared in advance. Although we observed only the physical spaces
of the shop, not the movement or behaviour of customers, we nonetheless
undertook a form of participant observation, in the sense that we are part of the
book-buying public in Tasmania, and already familiar with several of our sites
from past visits, and indeed, with bookstores in the state that are not part of our
sample. Like Ann Steiner in her observations of Swedish chain bookshops, we
recognised ourselves in this sense as 'material-gathering tool[s], although
hardly … objective one[s]'.[100] The insights we gleaned from our interviews
with booksellers and observations of their shops are discussed in the subsections
that follow, which relate respectively to the global bestseller in the local bookshop; the role of the local bestseller; and the relationship between curation and
in-store browsing.

2.3 'We Give Our Space to the Books': Localising the Bestseller
In a book retail market located on an island in a remote corner of the world,
the bestseller is both more *and* less influential than it might be in more

---

[99] D. Fuller, *Writing the Everyday: Women's Textual Communities in Atlantic
Canada*. (McGill-Queen's Press, 2004), p.18. See also Wilkin, Driscoll and
Fletcher, *Genre Worlds*, pp. 23–24.

[100] Steiner, 'Select, sell, display', 20.

central locations. Quixotic Books' Toby Wools-Cobb explained that a position on the 'end of the logistical network of supply and trade' typically creates an 'emphasis on the bestseller' because the higher costs that this end-of-the-line location generates make it more economical to send large quantities of fast-selling stock. On the other hand, the peripheral nature of the local market means that publishers put little effort into promoting their bestsellers there compared to metropolitan locations: '[They]'re really not too fussed about what happens in rural, regional Tasmania', observed Tim Gott at Devonport Bookshop: 'We're not the core business.'

In all cases, however, the local independent bookshops understood their identities in relation to bestsellers, even if this was premised on entirely ignoring them. The bookshops we focused on fell into three broad groups in relationship to global bestsellers: those in which they are a recognised staple, taking on a tentpole function (Not Just Books; Devonport Bookshop; Petrarch's); those in which they are closer to a necessary evil, required in small numbers to meet customer expectations but not whole-heartedly embraced (Fullers, The Hobart Bookshop); and those which defined themselves, explicitly or implicitly, against bestsellers (Black Swan; Quixotic).

The tentpole function of bestsellers within independent bookshops is well recognised. Miller notes that 'Popular sellers were once the bread and butter that supported many independents' less profitable selections. Now that market has largely been lost to the chains and warehouse clubs'.[101] Undertaking ethnographic research five years later (in the UK rather than the US), O'Brien nonetheless observed this dynamic persisting: 'the shop taps into whatever book genres, titles and authors are trending but . . . also curates a selection of less popular books that tend to sell in low numbers'.[102] Several of our booksellers spoke similarly: 'You need that core of bestsellers to give you a certain degree of cashflow', explained Gott from Devonport Bookshop. Although he recognised that, with the rise of DDSs, numbers of sales of bestsellers in independent bookshops had decreased, the category remained important: 'I still need those titles to give me my ten or twelve,

---

[101] Miller, *Reluctant Capitalists*, p. 149.
[102] O'Brien, 'Small and slow is beautiful', 580.

fifteen, particularly in that initial burst of activity – in those first three to four weeks of it being released.' While Gott, like others, acknowledged that DDSs 'down the road' would sell the same volume at around half the cost, he noted that this did not deter customers from purchasing it at his bookshop:

> For whatever reason, we don't seem to have been badly affected in terms of losing sales to either the internet or the Kmart. I think that may be because people know I keep a very good selection of the backlist. A lot of people will buy the new one. They enjoy it so much they want to read all the others . . . You may not always find the backlist up at the Kmart.

Another reason that some customers buy books from an independent bookshop, despite the higher price, is identity. A customer's sense that their taste or cultural position is reflected and catered to more by some retailers than others. Alexander Okenyo highlighted the connection between store and customer identity when explaining the origins of his bookshop's name: 'It was either going to be called Black Swan Bookshop or Town Square, because we're just on the town square. Very local, which speaks to curation and the individual identity of bookshops.' Tim Jarvis at Fullers shared that 'We . . . just pick up the . . . type of person who would prefer to buy that [globally bestselling] book from a bookshop. We just get the very margins of the sales on that kind of thing.' Although Fullers has sections labelled by genre ('Crime', 'Sci Fi + Fantasy'), it has only recently conceded the existence of the highest selling of all genres globally, romance. A group of comedy romances, many with cartoon covers popular on BookTok (like *Book Lovers*), occupies four lower shelves in the centre of the store, but there is no sign identifying this section, suggesting a certain reluctance to own this particularly popular genre. The Hobart Bookshop's approach is similar. With the shop's brand closely tied to its arts and tourist precinct location, the bestseller is less a staple than something tolerated: 'I won't not stock, but I don't have stacks of it.' Bronwyn Chalke's choice of word here is telling, as bestsellers are typically placed in literal stacks. Stock must go somewhere, and, away from walls, vertical space is often more available than floor area, but these stacks also increase the books' visibility, and send a message of volume to the customer, for better or worse. Chris Vitagliano from Not Just Books explains:

> When we get our new releases, so things like the Child, James Patterson – when you walked in, you would have seen that pyramid at the front – that's where the majority go. The ones that I buy the huge quantities of will go there. The other ones that I just buy two or three of to see how they will go, go on that wall

(see Figure 7). For some independent booksellers, homogeneous stacks are a pragmatic concession to the need for reliable sales; for

Figure 7 A mixture of international and national, fiction and non-fiction, bestsellers sit in stacks, topped by face-out copies, on the stand at the front of Not Just Books in Burnie.

others, they represent – to borrow Miller's phrase – 'an attack on the dignity of the book'.[103]

All the booksellers we interviewed were unified, however, in the view that while readers will find their own way to bestsellers, they needed guidance to discover interesting lower-profile books. Andy Durkin at Petrarch's told us, '[W]e know about bestsellers – but we handsell stuff that might get overlooked.' Similarly, she explained that publishers' promotional material was deprioritised and pushed to the edge of the shop: '[O]n the floor, we don't have a lot of space because we give our space to the books.' Quixotic Books makes its indifference to bestsellers a selling point in itself: according to its website, it gives customers the chance to 'discover books beyond the same bestseller names'.[104] Okenyo (Black Swan) admitted much the same:

> Opening a bookshop in a small, rural town at the edge of the world, it's not obvious that it'll work at all ... When I decided to open the shop, I said to myself, I'm not going to [focus on bestsellers] ... I don't need to earn very much money. I don't have a very expensive lifestyle. Then, it was like, I'm just going to see if I can do this the way I want to.

Quixotic and Black Swan epitomise what Miller terms the 'independent bookseller's stand against a mass society dominated by standardized mass culture'.[105]

Because our second case study focuses on a globally successful bestselling series, Child's Jack Reacher novels, we were interested in how this series functioned in local independent bookstores. Our interview and observation data on the series largely reflected our findings for global bestsellers in general. Some shops welcomed the predictability of each new title, promoting it while also keeping a large backlist. Not Just Books buys copies of the latest Reacher 'in bulk' and displays them in

---

[103] Miller, *Reluctant Capitalists*, p. 97.

[104] 'So then there was a bookshop', *Quixotic*, www.quixoticbooks.com.au/about.

[105] Miller, *Reluctant Capitalists*, p. 98.

Figure 8 The Jack Reacher series takes up a lot of shelf space in Devonport Bookshop.

stacks at the front of the store. For Petrarch's, the Reacher series is 'a reliable seller. I know how much I need', explains Durkin, 'I know who's buying it'. In the Devonport Bookshop, Child's novels took up a whole mid-height shelf, with two backlist titles face-out when we visited (see Figure 8). Gott concluded that, while other writers such as Nora Roberts and James Patterson sold very well, 'we probably haven't got anyone quite like Lee Child'. Others, by contrast, saw Child's bestsellers as tangential to their mission. At Fullers, 'they don't go gangbusters for us, but you know reliably that you'll sell a goodly number'. The Hobart Bookshop did not consider the novels to be bestsellers at all in the context of the store, although they keep the current title and one or two backlist titles. When we visited, a few Childs were unceremoniously squeezed, spine-out, against the end of a shelf, taking up no more room than the nearby Agatha Christies and Raymond Chandlers – Chalke noted that the shop's taste in crime is more 'vintagey'. Locality is a key part of The Hobart Bookshop's identity, situated as it is in a tourist, arts and historical precinct, and the Reacher brand – global but also strongly American, with its transitory, well-muscled, and diner-loving hero – simply doesn't fit this identity. Black Swan and Quixotic were both, proudly, Reacher-free zones.

Our analysis thus far has focused on the international bestseller in Tasmanian independent bookshops. But for most of the interviewees, this is a secondary way in which the term 'bestseller' functions. Its primary meaning is a localised one, in which the state, or the town, or the shop itself creates 'bestsellers', which in turn shape the bookshop.

2.4 'Bless Our Hearts . . . We Are Remarkably Parochial': *The Local Bestseller*

Although we sent our questions to booksellers in advance to help them structure their thoughts, we deliberately did not define the bestseller – an ambiguity our interviewees also embraced. As Wools-Cobb observed, '[T]here's no real criteria [for the bestseller] . . . Even if you do the criteria of a book selling so many, it'll be, "It was the highest sold book in this particular region in this particular month".' The booksellers were highly fluid in their use of the term, naming up international or global bestsellers (crime novelists James Patterson, David Baldacci, Daniel Silva, and Ann Cleeves were all mentioned); national bestsellers (such as titles by Jane Harper and Fiona McIntosh); local bestsellers (two Tasmanian authors, Robbie Arnott and Kyle Perry, both of whose most recent novels are set in the state, were mentioned by the majority of interviewees, with Danielle Wood/Minnie Darke, Meg Bignell, and Heather Rose also named multiple times); and even what might be termed hyper-local bestsellers (a non-fiction book by New Norfolk author Sam George-Allen was one of the highest sellers in Black Swan). Sales figures for books labelled 'bestsellers' by these bookshops could have sold anything from millions of copies globally to ten in the shop itself.

Although the booksellers considered the term 'bestseller' highly extensible, they embraced it most happily when it was applied at the regional or local level. 'Bless our hearts in Tasmania', said Gott, 'we are remarkably parochial.' Bronwyn Chalke noted that '[W]hat the national bestseller list is doesn't look anything like what my personal results are, and which books sell best for us.' Jarvis confirmed that Fullers's bestselling fiction list has become increasingly Tasmanian in flavour; of the shop's top ten bestsellers (fiction and non-fiction) current when we spoke to him, eight were Tasmanian, one Australian and one international (Delia Owen's *Where the Crawdads Sing*). The shop structures its new-book shelves (fiction and non-fiction) near the front of the store according to its internal bestseller list (see Figure 9), and displays for local bestsellers, with piles on pedestals, occupy a good proportion of the window space. Defined in this way, the bestseller is for most of the bookshops a concept they constantly utilise. Not Just Books has 'a TV screen out the front' promoting 'what's selling in our store'. Even Black Swan Bookshop was happy to feature 'the new Robbie Arnott . . . in [the] face-out section in the centre' of the shop, where Okenyo puts his 'things that [he] want[s] to sell'. Only Quixotic resisted the bestseller even on the local level, with Wools-Cobb never buying more than two or three copies of any one title.

Moreover, the local bestseller did not, by necessity, need to be set locally or even written by a local author. Jarvis noted that *This is Happiness*, a novel by Irish author Niall Williams, is 'constantly' on the Fullers bestseller list: 'We've sold, I'm told, squillions of copies . . . So far as I can tell, we're the only place in Australia where everybody cares about it. Everybody who reads the book recommends it to a few of their friends' (see Figure 9). The communities of readers created by the local bookshop through reading groups, newsletters, and other forms of collective engagement with books are then a key force that creates local bestsellers.

The sense of a local community centred on local or idiosyncratic bestsellers is part of the independent bookshop's appeal as a cosy, homely,

Figure 9 Fullers uses its internal bestseller list to structure the display of titles on its most prominent shelves. A local bestseller by a local author, Robbie Arnott's *Limberlost*, and a local bestseller by a non-local author, Niall Williams's *This is Happiness*, occupy the top two spots.

personalised environment.[106] As Chalke noted, 'As much as possible, we try to know what we are selling.' This intimate approach is taken to its extreme at Black Swan, where the titles on offer are largely an expression of the bookseller's taste: 'I buy in the shop as if I'm going to take it home', says Okenyo: 'That's how I select things.' Any piles of books that sit on this bookshop's surfaces are not multiple copies of the same title – high

[106] On the appeal of independent bookshops, see: Li, 'Choosing the right battles', 247–62; Laing and Royle, 'Examining chain bookstores', 27–44; O'Brien, 'Small and slow is beautiful', 573–95.

volume, low choice – but are rather heterogeneous and seemingly random, stacked as they might be in someone's home. This sense of entering a home as much as a shop – or both simultaneously – is reinforced by a lack of separation between books and food. In Black Swan, titles on cooking and wine rub up against bottles of locally made coffee liqueur, barrel-aged wild raspberry cider, and a pinot from a nearby winery. John Le Carré novels can be found inches from the café's choc-chip biscuits (see Figure 10).

When bestsellers are understood as the creation of local communities, the perceived opposition between the physical and online environments evident in our survey becomes less marked. Fullers lists its bestsellers in

Figure 10 Heterogeneous piles of books on the café counter in Black Swan Bookshop. Titles from the Loeb Classical Library, rubbing shoulders with John Le Carré novels, sit underneath the (excellent) chocolate-chip biscuits.

newsletters and promotes titles through its website and social media. Okenyo considers Instagram, where he frequently posts images of books, 'a massively important tool' for his bookshop, which 'punches above weight' in this regard due to its 'strong identity'. He believes that, given its out-of-the-way location, Black Swan 'would not work without social media'. Petrarch's favours Facebook, and notes that its website, which was created during COVID lockdowns to enable customers to purchase books, allows locals who have moved away to continue their allegiance. Seen as commercial and homogenising in relation to the global bestseller, virtual spaces flow easily into physical ones when it comes to the local bestseller.

One of the key reasons why our survey respondents preferred physical to online environments was the ability to browse. In the next section, we explore the way that browsing, curation, and the bestseller sit in relation to, and sometimes in tension with, each other.

2.5 'It's a Browsing Logic': Curating for Serendipity in the Bookshop

When we asked booksellers about the factors influencing the spatial display of bestsellers in their shops, most mentioned well-known techniques, such as stacking bestsellers near the front of the store and placing titles face-out on shelves. More interesting was what bestsellers were implicitly or explicitly understood against. Quixotic's website issues the promise of 'gems' to be found 'through serendipitous discovery'.[107] Wools-Cobb told us, '[T]here's an amount of people that come in with a breath of relief that they are seeing titles in my bookshop that they've never seen anywhere else. I think that's quite conducive to a retail atmosphere where people will kind of go, "I want to browse because I'm seeing things that aren't at the airport bookshop".' This opposition between browsing and global bestsellers frequently arose, if not always so explicitly, in our interviews.

Browsing is associated with a non-instrumental, leisurely, casual way of viewing a selection – indeed, one regional meaning of the word is 'to stroll

---

[107] 'So then there was a bookshop', www.quixoticbooks.com.au/about.

or wander aimlessly'.[108] Piles of the same small number of globally bestselling titles, by contrast, funnel the reader towards specific choices. The further the booksellers we interviewed distanced themselves from bestsellers, the more they emphasised this browsing function in their store layouts. Durkin explains, 'We divide our bookshop [Petrarch's] into sections ... to make little discovery pockets ... We literally plan our layout so that you have to weave in and out – you have to have a look. It's very visual. The experience of browsing in a bookshop is part of the discovery.' And while readers at The Hobart Bookshop – and most of the bookshops we visited – were guided by labels indicating genre, as well as the alphabetisation of titles by author, Quixotic Books eschews conventional retail display: its historical fiction titles, for example, are ordered according to period. Wools-Cobb emphasised the shop's 'browsing logic – it's serendipitous'. At Black Swan, there are no labels at all. While insisting that 'it's not as random as it looks' – titles are shelved alphabetically, at least – Okenyo admits, 'As a person who loves bookshops, I also like a little bit of: if you're not going to the exact place that you came thinking you wanted to go to, you might stumble across something ... Not having things so clearly labelled allows [that].' Within the 'browsing logic' of the independent bookshop, the bestseller is the antithesis to serendipitous discovery: you cannot 'stumble' upon something that is everywhere. The bestseller signifies volume and sameness; browsing evokes heterogeneity, diversity, and unpredictability.

This binary becomes less straightforward, however, when the idea of curation is introduced. Previous scholars have emphasised the importance of curation in independent bookshops. O'Brien, for example, observes that 'Curatorship of a personally selected, small range of books holds value for customers', as does a sense of 'happy surprise'.[109] Our interviews reinforced these findings: the more Tasmanian bookshops valued serendipity, the more they used curation to ensure this quality. The bookseller used his or her individual taste and knowledge to choose and arrange stock to simultaneously surprise and delight the customer. Serendipity, then, is produced for the shopper by the stock as well as the spatial layout of the store;

---

[108] 'Browse', *Oxford English Dictionary*, www-oed-com.ezproxy.utas.edu.au/view/Entry/23882.

[109] O'Brien, 'Small and slow is beautiful', 588, 586.

paradoxically, they are guided towards the unexpected. In the same way, by shopping at an independent rather than a DDS, or a chain in a shopping centre, the shopper is making a purposive choice of serendipity. Okenyo explains of Black Swan,

> 'The thing about being in the city is, you just have foot traffic, which I don't have. People have to come here ... I think there's something special about it being here. I think it would get lost in a city, whereas here it feels really special, and people just come and drive through the country, along the river.'

Those who visit Black Swan, then, do not just stumble upon it: they choose to make the drive, in order to stumble upon books.

In her study of Swedish bookshops, Steiner argues that bestseller lists are a form of curation and also 'create a sense of community with other readers', although she also observes resistance to the idea that these lists should be 'one of many tools that bookshops use to guide their customers'.[110] Based on our data, we argue that while this might be true of the global bestseller, local bestseller lists are a form of curation embraced by independent bookshops – a way of guiding readers towards titles that the local community itself considers worthwhile. This form of curation is reinforced in three of the seven bookshops we visited by shelf talkers written by staff, which are sometimes also shared on social media channels. Jarvis (Fullers) claimed that 'when they really work, [shelf talkers] can create a bestseller'. Usually attributed to a staff member by their first name (and sometimes a group of staff), shelf talkers reinforced the sense of intimacy already inherent in the curation of independent bookshops' handpicked stock. Certainly, local titles were strongly recommended in this way: 'an amazing Tassie talent' (referring to Arnott), 'Bravo to local talent' (referring to Hobart-based Katherine Johnson).[111] In some cases, being local was the whole of the recommendation ('Tasmanian author!'; 'Local author, local story. Only $9.95'[112]). However, shelf talkers could be found attached to all manner of

---

[110] Steiner, 'Select, display, and sell', 26.
[111] Shelf talkers at Petrarch's (5 September 2022). [112] Ibid.

titles including global bestsellers, giving them the imprimatur of local recommendation. For example, although Child readers are 'not necessarily looking for the handsell', Child's novels received their share of shelf talkers ('Another page turning adventure in the usual Jack Reacher style. Fans will not be disappointed'),[113] and provided a reference point for other titles ('perfect for fans of Lee Child!!'[114]). Child is more popular than Patterson at Fullers, Jarvis speculates, because 'we have had staff who are quite keen on Jack Reacher'. Bestsellers, then, may be the antithesis of browsing, but they are very much the product of communal curation – curation that occurs in different ways for different purposes and on different scales, but often involves the intersection of the local and the global.

The bestseller is simultaneously a slippery, ambiguous category and one that inspires strong, even passionate responses, both positive and negative. Themselves understood spatially as 'big' books (one interviewee used this word to describe them[115]), bestsellers are viewed as in many ways taking up too much room, crowding out other deserving titles – except when they are local, in which case they are considered deserving and community-enhancing rather than homogenising. While most of the bookshops we spoke to were sanguine enough about the global bestseller to feature stacks out the front of their shops, this was a concession that enabled them to concentrate on their central mission of introducing readers to deserving local or lower-profile titles. While discerning selection and arrangement of stock – curation – was important, equally important was the unexpected find, and indeed bookshops arranged their layouts partly to orchestrate such accidents. Perhaps surprisingly, a similar tension between deliberate choice and serendipitous encounter characterises the globally bestselling series to which we now turn.

---

[113] Andy Durkin (Petrarch's Bookshop), personal interview; shelf talker at Devonport Bookshop (8 September 2022).

[114] Shelf talker, Petrarch's.

[115] Bronwyn Chalke (The Hobart Bookshop), personal interview.

3 The Reach of the Bestseller

In this section, we examine Lee Child's action-thriller series, Jack Reacher, to show how a focus on spatiality makes visible the connections between the textual and industrial layers of bestselling novels. We argue that Reacher's adventures reveal and explore tensions between overlapping spatial concepts (local and global, random movement and linear progress, serendipity and algorithm) that are at the heart of the bestseller as text and commercial product. These tensions are paralleled in the marketing and circulation of the series, which we demonstrate through a consideration of how Reacher and Reacher books inhabit and move through the digital sphere. Reading this series with a focus on space and place enables us to understand how the textual, industrial, and social are always imbricated in novels that are marketed, sold, and read under the banner of 'bestsellers'.

Centred on its titular ex-military cop turned drifter, the Reacher series began with the release of *The Killing Floor* in 1997. Child then settled into a regular pattern of commencing the writing of a new title in September each year to be released in October of the following year. In this way, every year sees the publication of a new Reacher (the name is applied equally to character, title, and series), which reliably occupies top place on the *New York Times* bestseller list for fiction. Since 2020, Child has co-authored the Reacher novels with his brother Andrew as a way of easing into retirement without his hero needing to stop his wandering. Film adaptations in 2012 and 2016, and an Amazon Prime television series launched in February 2022, reinforced the already dominant Reacher brand. In June 2022, Amazon.co.uk released combined ebook and print sales data, identifying Jack Reacher as their bestselling book series of all time.[116] Worldwide, the series – comprising twenty-eight novels (complemented by several short stories) translated into over forty languages – has generated sales of over 100 million copies.[117] This is

[116] S. Bayley, 'Jack Reacher beats Harry Potter as Amazon reveals bestselling book series', *The Bookseller* (23 June 2022), www.thebookseller.com/news/jack-reacher-beats-harry-potter-as-amazon-reveals-bestselling-book-series.

[117] E. Latimer, 'Home and home-less: Narrating and negating the domestic in contemporary crime fiction series', *Clues*, 39 (2021), 72. See also, R. Barber, 'Lee Child: The man who's sold 100 million books', *Stuff* (5 April 2017), www.stuff

a large number, but it actually places Reacher behind megaselling series that have generated higher sales with significantly fewer volumes: J. K. Rowling's Harry Potter with more than 500 million copies sold, E. L. James's Fifty Shades of Grey with over 160 million copies, and Dan Brown's Robert Langdon with over 120 million sales. Closer comparisons to Reacher include James Patterson's thirty-one-book Alex Cross series and Robert Jordan's fifteen-book Wheel of Time (continued from book 13 by Brandon Sanderson following Jordan's death), which both boast sales of over 100 million copies, and J. D. Robb's (aka Nora Roberts) sixty-three-book In Death series with over 66 million sales.[118]

The tagline on the inside front cover of the Bantam Press edition of *61 Hours* (2010), the fourteenth book in the series, asks 'If you don't know Jack Reacher, where have you been?' Here, Reacher, as doubly character and type of book, epitomises the everywhere-ness of the bestseller, an expansive and exploratory attribute that is at once textual and industrial. The question floats in yellow font above a wintry landscape featuring a jet silhouetted in a stormy sky and a dark SUV taking an icy curve. Child stands in the foreground, almost filling the page, hands buried in the pockets of a long, black coat. He looks relaxed and thoughtful, but also rugged, a little tense, and very tall. The photograph highlights Child's lined face, the creases of a slight frown on his forehead, and his thin, pressed-together lips. He is not smiling, nor is he looking at the camera, which would be more typical for an

.co.nz/entertainment/books/91106765/lee-child-the-man-whos-sold-100-million-books; J. Moody, '100 million copies, a sale every NINE seconds and 61 weeks at No1: The remarkable stats behind the Jack Reacher series', *Mirror* (3 April 2018), www.mirror.co.uk/news/uk-news/100-million-copies-sale-every-12259882; 'Jack Reacher author Lee Child passes writing baton to brother', *BBC News* (18 January 2020), www.bbc.com/news/entertainment-arts-51162838.

[118] Finding accurate and consistent data for book sales is a dark art. The figures offered here are based on a synthesis of multiple news reports for each series, recognising that many of these are fed by publishers' and/or booksellers' media releases. Estimates of sales are included here to situate the Reacher series in relation to others series that circulate as bestsellers and have gathered the commercial and cultural force to shape the category in the twenty-first century.

author photograph. Instead, Child looks to the sky, as though he is waiting for
the plane to fly overhead or, perhaps, dreaming up Reacher's next adventure; the
line of his gaze also points towards the yellow tagline. Child is dressed similarly
to the small figure on the bottom left of the front cover who walks away from the
viewer, his hands in his pockets against the bitter cold. It is almost as though the
author photo is a close-up reveal of the man on the cover; Child and Reacher
stand, walk, and fly together, an author/hero doubling that is central to the series
marketing. The everywhere-ness of this bestseller is a function of the fusing of
author and hero in a single brand identity; the expansive and penetrative market
power of this bestselling series is two-pronged.[119]

The mirroring of the living author and the fictional drifter is evident also in
the review extracts on the inside front cover. The first is from Kenneth Turan's
Los Angeles Times review of *Gone Tomorrow* (2009), the thirteenth book in the
series:

> Expert at ratcheting up the **tension** ... the folks he deals
> with consistently underestimate him ... You want to **scream**
> at them, 'This is **Jack Reacher** for pity's sake, he'll **eat you**
> for breakfast!' He will, you know, and that's why we keep
> coming back for more.[120]

In the full review, the first phrase, 'expert at ratcheting up the tension',
refers to Child's achievement of a 'propulsive' writing style; the second, 'the
folks he deals with consistently underestimate him', refers to Reacher. The
extract runs the quotations together so that it is not clear if the reviewer is
praising Reacher or Child, conflating author and character.

The conflation of Child and Reacher is intensified by another paratextual element on some copies of this edition of *61 Hours*. A sticker on

[119] This cover design is repeated for other titles, including *The Affair*. (Bantam,
2011) and *Worth Dying For*. (Bantam, 2010).

[120] Original emphasis, L. Child, *61 Hours*. (Bantam, 2010), inside front cover. For
full review, see K. Turan, 'The Thrill is Back (So is Reacher)', *Los Angeles
Times* (19 May 2009), www.latimes.com/archives/la-xpm-2009-may-19-et-
book19-story.html.

the front cover promotes a competition with the words, 'Win $5000. Are you Jack Reacher?' The sticker directs consumers to a now-defunct website promoting the Australian round of a worldwide search for a Reacher doppelgänger – www.areyoujackreacher.com.au. The winner, Duncan Munro, also won the international final in San Francisco, where he met Child.[121] Munro then appeared as Reacher at Random House events to promote the Australian release of *The Affair* (2011), a novel that features a character called Duncan Munro who looks and thinks like Reacher: 'Who else was authorised to be out and about? He even looked like me. Same kind of height, same kind of build, similar colouring. It was like looking in a mirror . . .' Reacher and Munro connect immediately, a simpatico relationship that evokes the dynamics of character identification or relatability that the competition sought to activate: '"Great minds think alike," Munro said. "Or fools never differ."'[122] The bestseller both seeks to be world-embracing and to be a world unto itself, lassoing author, character, and millions of readers into a shared imaginary through the business of books.

3.1 The Academics Said Nothing

Despite having sold more than 100 million copies over more than a quarter of a century, the Jack Reacher novels – like other enormously popular series – have attracted very little attention from academic critics. Significant exceptions include Andy Martin's two books, *Reacher Said Nothing: Lee Child and the Making of MAKE ME* (2015) – the first part of the title riffing off a phrase that appears dozens of times in the series – and *With Child: Lee Child and the Readers of Jack Reacher* (2019). In *Reacher Said Nothing*, Martin recounts the experience of literally sitting in Child's study and detailing the process whereby he produces a novel once a year.[123] In its sequel, Martin observes the promotion and reception of the twentieth novel in the series, *Make Me* (2015), travelling

---

[121] S. Nesdale, 'Jack Reacher Look-a-Like Competition Winner: Duncan Munro', *LoveJackReacher*.com (25 March 2014), www.lovejackreacher.com/jack-reacher-look-a-like-competition-winner-duncan-munro/.

[122] Child, *The Affair*. (Bantam, 2011), p. 287.

[123] A. Martin, *Reacher Said Nothing: Lee Child and the Making of Make Me*. (Bantam, 2015).

with Child on the book circuit.[124] While Martin pays very close attention to words on the page (or rather screen, as Child writes on a computer), these two studies are not conventional works of academic criticism.

Other than Martin's two chatty, irreverent, and innovative analyses of the series' creation and reception, our searches have turned up only a single book chapter and four journal articles – one of them an analysis of Reacher's leadership style published in the *Journal of Management and Organization*.[125] Most directly relevant to our spatial analysis is historical geographer Philip Howell's 'Jack Reacher's carbon footprint: Reading airport novels irresponsibly.'[126] While Howell's 'carbon accounting' of a fictional character – including a map of Reacher's flights and a table listing his CO_2 emissions from 1974 to 2020^{127} – is offered as 'sort of satire on the more literal [ecocritical] treatments of environmental responsibility', his analysis of air travel in the Reacher series is presented as a serious contribution 'towards understanding the literary geography of thrillers like these, the kind of thing that gets dismissed as "airport fiction," and thus wholly ignored'.[128] For our purposes, Howell's analysis reinforces the importance of spatiality to the series: '[T]here's just such a lot of *geography* to like in the Reacher novels, even when you don't know precisely where the action is set.'[129] At the level of the text, Howell agrees, attention to place is a key component of the series.

While none of the other analyses of the series that we identified are strongly interested in space and place, they all touch on questions relevant to our focus on bestsellers. Elizabeth Blakesley makes a case for taking Reacher seriously, but only inasmuch as the series transcends its bestselling status: 'Although the Reacher series has not yet received scholarly scrutiny,

---

[124] A. Martin, *With Child: Lee Child and the Readers of Jack Reacher*. (Polity, 2019).

[125] R. Bathurst and A. Crystall, 'Attending *Night School*: Leadership lessons at the Jack Reacher academy', *Journal of Management and Organization*, 25 (2019), 430–44.

[126] P. Howell, 'Jack Reacher's carbon footprint: Reading airport novels irresponsibly', *Literary Geographies*, 8 (2022), 19–44.

[127] These amount to 79 flights, covering 282,240 airmiles producing 22 tonnes of CO_2. Howell, 'Jack Reacher's carbon footprint', 32.

[128] Ibid., 26, 29. [129] Ibid., 35.

the novels are more than just best-selling beach reads.'[130] Taking the worthiness of popular fiction for granted, Jeroen Vermeulen focuses on genre, arguing that Reacher 'straddles two emblematic American genres – cowboy and hard-boiled fiction – in his quest for absolute, utopian freedom'.[131] Lee Mitchell, examining Child's novels along with the television series *24* as examples of the contradictions inherent in popular narratives, also considers the question of Reacher's freedom, although in this case in terms of technology and surveillance.[132]

We draw on all these previous analyses in this section. As this summary shows, however, on the whole, literary critics have ignored Child, as they have largely ignored other massively successful action-thriller authors, such as James Patterson, Clive Cussler, David Baldacci, and Michael Connelly.[133] This neglect is not simply a product of literary studies' bias against popular fiction, but is likely also due to the methodological challenges of considering multiple titles simultaneously, and through the lens of popular rather than literary fiction – that is, paying attention to industry-based factors in conjunction with the text itself. Our analysis seeks a way of reading from the 'middle distance': building on close knowledge of individual titles but treating the series as a simultaneously textual, social, and industrial phenomenon. This approach allows us to better understand the spatial logic of this bestselling series and to extrapolate from our observations to bestsellers more broadly.

---

[130] E. Blakesley, 'Lee Child's pure, uncomplicated hero' in G. Hoppenstand (ed.), *Critical Insights: The American Thriller*. (Salem Press, 2014), pp. 95–96.

[131] J. Vermeulen, 'The lonely road to freedom: Jack Reacher's interpretation of an American myth', *Clues: A Journal of Detection*, 35 (2017), 113.

[132] L. Mitchell, 'Fairy tales and thrillers: The contradictions of formula narratives', *Literary Imagination*, 11 (2009), 278–90.

[133] Exceptions include: R. Crane and L. Fletcher, 'The Proximity of islands: Dirk Pitt's insular adventures' in R. Crane and L. Fletcher (eds.), *Island Genres, Genre Islands: Conceptualisation and Representation in Popular Fiction*. (Rowman & Littlefield International, 2017), pp. 71–84 which focuses on Cussler's most famous series; C. Gregoriou, *Deviance in Contemporary Crime Fiction*. (Palgrave Macmillan, 2007), which features case studies of Connelly and Patterson; and J. Hermes, 'Of irritation, texts and men: Feminist audience studies and cultural citizenship', *International Journal of Cultural Studies*, 3 (2000), 351–67, which briefly discusses Baldacci's 1997 novel *Total Control*.

3.2 'All Over the Place': The Reach of Reacher

'A Jack Reacher book is sold somewhere in the world every NINE SECONDS.'[134] Although the number of seconds varies (at some points plummeting to four and at others climbing as high as twenty), this claim about Jack Reacher – made here in the *Mirror* newspaper – is routinely repeated in the media when the series is discussed. This emphasis on rapid sales parallels the speed of action that is a hallmark of the thriller – endorsements tout them as 'fast-paced', 'pulseracing', and 'dynamic'.[135] But the familiar claim says as much about the geographic span as the temporal rhythm of Child's sales: 'somewhere in the world' suggests that Child's readership is not confined to any one location but embraces the whole globe. Indeed, the *Mirror* follows the nine-second claim by stating that 'The Jack Reacher books are published in over 100 territories worldwide ... You know that well-known saying that you're never more than six foot away from a spider? Well, the same can be said for Jack Reacher fans.'[136] The message is consistent across the paratext: 'If you don't know Jack Reacher, where have you been?'[137]

Just as the fast sales reflect the pace of action within the series, the spatial ubiquity of its success parallels the geographical restlessness of its protagonist. The eponymous hero is famously a drifter who rarely stays in any one location for more than ten days, sleeps mostly in cheap motels, and owns nothing but a passport, a credit card, a toothbrush, and the clothes he wears – which he discards when he needs a change, buying a new set and

---

[134] Moody, '100 million copies'.

[135] Endorsements from versions of the Bantam editions of *Never Go Back* (2014), *Personal* (2015) and *The Enemy* (2005).

[136] Moody, '100 million copies'.

[137] Reacher's reach is extended by Diane Capri's 20-book series, The Hunt for Jack Reacher, which began in 2012 with *Don't Know Jack*. Capri's website proclaims her a '*New York Times* and *USA Today* bestselling author', with an endorsement from Lee Child top-of-page: 'Full of thrills and tension – but smart and human too'. In the series, 'FBI Special Agent Kim Otto picks up where Lee Child leaves off in the Hunt for Jack Reacher' https://dianecapri.com/books/hunt-jack-reacher-series/.

throwing the old ones in the bin.[138] He is 'Geographically, all over the place, literally. Forty states and counting in five years'.[139] For Elspeth Latimer, Reacher's homelessness exemplifies the 'lack of investment in the domestic environment in much contemporary crime fiction'.[140] Although Reacher's peregrinations are concentrated in the US, the action of the series sees him travel (in flashback or present time) to the UK, France, Germany, Japan, and Australia. His time serving in Iraq is inscribed on his body, in the form of a shrapnel scar on his torso. He has lived on six continents, including in a weather hut in Antarctica and an air force base in Greenland.

Alongside his imposing height and prodigious skills as a streetfighter, then, one of Reacher's key characteristics is his ceaseless mobility. Just as Reacher novels circulate globally and locally – more or less predictably – Reacher himself moves fluidly from small towns to urban metropolises, equally happy and competent in all these places, pausing only when a barrier appears in his path or his curiosity is piqued. His adeptness at moving his large body through diverse spaces (the backwoods of New England in *Past Tense* (2018), the boulevards of Paris in *Personal* (2014)) is central not only to his lifestyle but also his success as a crime-fighter – or rather, as the blurbs on the Bantam paperback editions insist, a 'righteous avenger'. To underline this mobility, Child sometimes introduces spaces with strange dimensions to which Reacher must adapt if he is to survive: in *Personal*, a house built 50 per cent bigger than usual proportions, to accommodate its six-foot-eleven occupant, the mobster Little Joey; and, in *61 Hours*, an underground shelter constructed for children, which suits Reacher's

---

[138] Howell's analysis of Reacher's environmental footprint mentions his lack of ownership of a house or belongings as contributors to his status as a fictional low-carbon exemplar. Reacher's constant discarding and buying of clothes, along with the extra laundry and cleaning that his motel-based lifestyle presumably entails, put this (admittedly already tongue-in-cheek) case for his pro-environmental credentials into doubt.

[139] L. Child, *Without Fail.* (Transworld Digital, 2008), p. 14. All page references to Reacher novels cited in this section, except where otherwise specified, are from Transworld Kindle editions.

[140] E. Latimer, 'Home and Home-Less', 74.

diminutive opponent, but cripples the hulking ex-MP. As an inveterate wanderer, Reacher finds enclosed spaces claustrophobic, and his worst fear is entrapment: '[H]e had known since his early boyhood that he was terrified of being trapped in the dark in a space too small to turn his giant frame. All his damp childhood nightmares had been about being closed into tight spaces.'[141] Reacher embodies a fantasy of spatial freedom, a portrayal that evokes the promise to readers of 'pure escapism'.[142]

While action thriller heroes tend to be highly mobile (think James Bond or Jack Ryan), Reacher's almost pathological restlessness makes the series intensely geographical. Reacher's childhood, moving between military bases across the world (his father was in the Marines), alongside the spatial strictures of his own career in the army – that 'vast worldwide fortress'[143] – means that, despite having travelled widely, he is effectively a stranger in his own country. When discharged from the army, Reacher continues the constant movement that characterised his service but reacts against its rigid linearity: he likens military life to 'rushing down a narrow corridor, eyes fixed firmly to the front'.[144] For this reason, although he continues to insist on always moving forward, he is determined to incorporate an element of randomness in his travels: 'conscious choice would turn drifting into something else completely. The whole point of drifting was happy passive acceptance of no alternatives.'[145] Thus, Reacher embraces unexpected 'detour[s]', 'whim[s]', 'crazy zigzags', and 'side trips'.[146] Ironically, he deliberately builds randomness into his life through his 'rules' – such as taking the first bus out of town that he encounters, even if its destination seems unappealing.[147]

---

[141] L. Child, *Die Trying*. (Transworld Digital, 2008), p. 405.

[142] Endorsement on L. Child, *A Wanted Man*. (Bantam, 2013).

[143] L. Child, *The Enemy*. (Bantam, 2005), cover blurb.

[144] L. Child, *The Visitor*. (Transworld Digital, 2008), p. 362.

[145] L. Child, *Tripwire*. (Transworld Digital, 2008), p. 342.

[146] L. Child, *Nothing to Lose*. (Transworld Digital, 2008), p. 4; Child, *The Visitor*, p. 362.

[147] For example: L. Child, *The Midnight Line*. (Transworld Digital, 2017), p. 2.

The transition point in Reacher's life is revealed at the end of *The Affair*, the novel that features Duncan Munro in its pages and promotion. *The Affair* flashes back to Reacher's earlier military experiences and is set in 1997, the year the first book in the series appeared. This novel explains some of the motivation behind Reacher's decision to leave the army and shows him learning the techniques (hitchhiking, living in motels, buying rather than washing clothes) that he later perfects as a drifter. At the novel's conclusion, after Reacher deposits a form with the Pentagon (presumably his departure paperwork), he reflects on the possibilities ahead:

> I was thirty-six years old, a citizen of a country I had barely seen, and there were places to go, and there were things to do. There were cities, and there was countryside. There were mountains, and there were valleys. There were rivers. There were museums, and music, and motels, and clubs, and diners, and bars, and buses. There were battlefields and birthplaces, and legends, and roads. There was company if I wanted it, and there was solitude if I didn't. I picked a road at random, and I put one foot on the kerb and one in the traffic lane, and I stuck out my thumb.[148]

Although this list suggests something of a sightseeing tour, Howell argues that Reacher's embrace of the mundane and everyday, rather than typical visitor attractions, means that, despite his incessant travel, he is best understood as 'an *antitourist*'.[149] Reacher himself is compared by one of his frustrated lovers to a holiday destination: '*You're like New York City. I love to visit, but I could never live there.*'[150] As a reading experience, a Reacher novel gives readers a brief but intense vacation of sorts in a world they would not want to inhabit. The curious adventures of Duncan Munro, Reacher and Child look-alike and fan, play explicitly with this fantasy of escape in the books' world (and the world of books). In an interview,

[148] L. Child, *The Affair*. (Transworld Digital, 2011), p. 405.
[149] Howell, 'Jack Reacher's carbon footprint', 34.
[150] Child, *The Midnight Line*, p. 1.

Munro (in costume as his namesake from *The Affair*) says that what he relates to most is Reacher's mobility: 'Lee has captured that wanderlust, that love for freedom that Reacher has. He never wants to stay too long in one place.'[151]

Yet the random drifting that characterises Reacher's lifestyle contrasts with a desire for onward, systematic progress. As with most crime thrillers, a mystery is solved by the end of the novel; the reader keeps turning the pages, and Reacher himself keeps moving ahead: 'Everyone's life needed an organizing principle, and relentless forward motion was Reacher's.'[152] And when it comes to solving crimes, like a thriller reader, Reacher is motivated by the fact that he 'just want[s] to find out what happened'.[153] At the level of the text, Reacher novels, like most thrillers, are structured to maximise a linear narrative drive – to keep the reader turning pages, to be 'unputdownable'. Thus, the reading experience of the bestseller could be likened to the blinkered military existence that Reacher, through his deliberate zigzagging, rejects.[154] The tension between predictability, repeatability, and linearity on the one hand, and randomness, emergence, and irregularity on the other, that characterises this bestselling series reflects something intrinsic to the bestseller as a commercial and cultural category.

3.3 Locating Reacher

When readers open a new book in the series, then, they can be confident of at least one thing: that Reacher will almost always have moved on from where they last encountered him.[155] Although he claims a preference for warmer climes,[156] his taste in location is catholic: the novels are set all over

---

[151] Meet Duncan Munro, Australia's Very Own Jack Reacher – *The* Affair, by Lee Child', *YouTube* (2 November 2011), www.youtube.com/watch?v=IfOEzBDhZsw.

[152] Child, *Nothing to Lose*, p. 7. [153] Child, *The Midnight Line*, p. 220.

[154] Child, *The Visitor*, p. 362.

[155] There are exceptions: Reacher spends longer than usual with the same woman in *The Midnight Line* and particularly *The Visitor*.

[156] For example: Child, *The Midnight Line*, p. 2.

the US, from a snow-covered South Dakota town to the 'deep ... New England woods'; from the 'wilds of Nebraska' to a ranch in the 'hellish heat of a Texan summer'.[157] The Penguin Random House website offers readers a choice between titles set 'in the city', those set 'overseas', and 'small town dramas'.[158] In some cases, the entire action happens within a very limited location (a good part of the narrative of *A Wanted Man* [2012] takes place in a moving car), while in others Reacher ranges across the American country-side or crosses international borders. Larger cities tend to be actual, named places, while the smaller towns are often fictional (although usually located within named states). Some invented names are seemingly random – for example, Carter Crossing, Mississippi, in *The Affair* – while others are ostentatiously portentous, such as Hope and Despair, Colorado, in *Nothing to Lose* (2008) or the ironic and non-fictional Pleasantville, Tennessee, in *The Sentinel* (2020). In *Make Me*, the whole action is triggered by the name of a town, Mother's Rest, to which Reacher diverts after becoming intrigued about its origins. Only rarely are places unnamed, as in *One Shot's* (2005) generic 'heartland city' in Indiana and the unspecified town in the eastern US in *Blue Moon* (2019).

Locations can also be playfully metafictional, such as Los Gemolos (The Twins) in *Better Off Dead* (2021), co-authored by Child and his novelist brother. An extended version of this blurring of places 'inside' and 'outside' of the text occurs in *The Midnight Line* (2017), in which a small West Point ring in a pawn shop in Wisconsin inspires Reacher to track down its owner, a search that takes him first to South Dakota and thence Wyoming. The latter is described in the novel as 'Reacher country', its appeal for him lying in its 'heroic geography', 'heroic climate', and 'emptiness'.[159] Wyoming is also Reacher country in another way: in the same year *The Midnight Line* was published, Child's brother Andrew moved to the state, with Lee later buying a nearby ranch and himself moving from New York to Wyoming.

[157] Child, *61 Hours*, cover blurb; L. Child, *Past Tense*. (Bantam, 2019), cover blurb; L. Child, *Worth Dying For*. (Bantam, 2010), cover blurb; L. Child, *Echo Burning*. (Bantam, 2011), cover blurb.

[158] 'Jack Reacher: US', *Penguin Random House*, www.jackreacher.com/us/.

[159] Child, *The Midnight Line*, p. 82.

The novel gestures to this parallel when the neighbour of a murdered man explains why there was no speculation about how the latter earned a living: 'We figured he was a rich guy from out of state, come to find himself. We get those, from time to time. Maybe they're writing a novel.'[160] Within Wyoming, Reacher's investigations point to the tiny town of Mule Crossing, the site of an old post office that has now been converted to a flea market, alongside a shop selling fireworks. While the location itself is fictional, a Reacher fan on Reddit writes that following the directions specified in the novel leads to the town of Tie Siding, where a sign advertising fireworks abuts a combined post office and flea market.[161] A search on Google Maps shows that roads called Elk Crossing and Deer Crossing are nearby. Real and imagined geographies are playfully blurred in the novel, reflecting Reacher's similarities to his creator.[162]

Although pivotal to the narratives, the settings are almost never mentioned in the novels' titles, which tend to emphasise actions, events, and sometimes time (*Blue Moon*, *Gone Tomorrow*, *61 Hours*, *Past Tense*). Echo County, Texas, in *Echo Burning* (2001) is the only exception, and even this is non-obvious as a place name to the new reader. However, place is certainly dominant in the cover blurbs and images. Many of the blurbs announce the setting in the first few words – 'From a helicopter high above the California desert'; 'New York City. Two in the morning'; 'There's deadly trouble in the corn country of Nebraska.'[163] Alternatively, they open by reinforcing Reacher's constant mobility: 'Reacher takes a stroll through a small Wisconsin town'; 'Jack Reacher hits the pavement and sticks out his

---

[160]   Ibid., p. 157.

[161]   Kenlin, 'r/JackReacher', *Reddit*, www.reddit.com/r/JackReacher/comments/ 8av1le/mule_crossing_wy/.

[162]   Martin suggests it is 'not unreasonable' to consider 'The hero is simply a more muscular avatar of the writer', although this equation is also 'naïve' because there are other, less attractive 'alter egos' in the novels. *With Child*, p. 256.

[163]   From blurbs attached to Bantam Books Trade Paperback Editions (displayed at: 'Jack Reacher series', *Penguin Random House*, www.penguinrandomhouse .com/series/JAC/jack-reacher/) of respectively *Bad Luck and Trouble* (2022), *Gone Tomorrow* (2012), and *Worth Dying for* (2012).

thumb. He plans to follow the sun on an epic trip across America, from Maine to California'; 'As always, Reacher has no particular place to go, and all the time in the world to get there.'[164] Almost every Penguin Random House cover for the series shows a lone tall man, usually with his back towards the viewer, standing on or walking along a road, with the background – an urban scene, a snow-covered church, a forest, a run-down motel – signifying a key location of the title.[165] Although the landscape or cityscape takes up most of the image, the masculine figure is normally positioned in the foreground and a significant object – church, motel – in the background, so that in terms of relative size they are about equal, just as Reacher is equal to any environment that he wanders into. With the road (or sometimes a railway) most often leading from the bottom of the image to a horizon someway up the page, it is as if the reader is being invited on a geographical as well as a textual journey, following Reacher into the space of the narrative. Perhaps the most striking example is the cover of *A Wanted Man*, in which the silhouette of a tall hitchhiker is positioned against a road that runs from the bottom right-hand corner towards a horizon low on the page, with the endorsement beneath promising 'Pure escapism' (see Figure 11). The reader opening the book, like Reacher sticking out his thumb, is asking to be transported. If a key expectation for readers buying fiction from a bookshop is 'An escape into another world', then the covers of Reacher novels target this need.[166]

While the matching covers, the conventions of the genre and the regularity of Reacher's ramblings can make the novels' settings seem

---

[164] From blurbs attached to Bantam Books Trade Paperback Editions (displayed at: 'Jack Reacher series', *Penguin Random House,* www.penguinrandomhouse .com/series/JAC/jack-reacher/) of respectively *The Midnight Line* (2018), *Past Tense* (2019), and *The Sentinel* (2021).

[165] This design standard is closely followed by the covers of Capri's piggyback Hunt for Jack Reacher series and is consistent with genre coding for masculinist action thrillers, including Patterson's Alex Cross series, David Baldacci's Amos Decker series, and the Tom Clancy's Jack Ryan thrillers written by Mark Greaney.

[166] S. Frost, 'Readers and retailed literature: Findings from a UK public high street survey of purchasers' expectations from books', *Logos*, 28 (2017), 32.

Figure 11 The Sainsbury's Book Club sticker might detract from the mythic weight of the scene on the cover of this Bantam 2013 edition of *A Wanted Man*. However, Reacher himself would no doubt appreciate this slightly grubby, pre-loved copy.

interchangeable, the specifics of the location are often central to the action. As Reacher remarks about (fictional) Margrave, Georgia, in *The Killing Floor*, 'It wasn't me against them, played out against a neutral background. The background wasn't neutral. The background was the opposition.'[167] The inevitability of a new setting for each adventure, together with the unique specificity of that setting, function like the conventions of popular fiction more generally to provide a balance

[167] L. Child, *The Killing Floor*. (Transworld Digital, 2009), p. 347.

between met expectation and novelty. This is the combination a character alludes to in *The Midnight Line* when she speculates to Reacher about why her twin sister chose a hideaway in Wyoming, where she spent her childhood: 'To have both is just right. Familiarity and unfamiliarity.'[168] This combination of convention and originality is exactly what is served to the reader in each Reacher novel, and arguably in all successful popular genre fiction.

3.4 Reading Places

As well as being an inveterate wanderer and a virtuoso fighter, Reacher is also a highly trained reader. His detective method relies heavily on his knowledge of places – both specific locations and generic ones. As Howell points out, despite his global jet-setting, Reacher 'is, wholly pleasingly, curiously attentive to the local'.[169] In New York, for example, he finds the hideout of the terrifying Svetlana and Lila Hoth because of his knowledge of 'the micro-geography of Manhattan' – realising, for example, that they are unlikely to have gone beyond the wide, busy 57th Street, which functions 'like the Mississippi River' as an 'obstacle', a 'boundary', a 'conceptual barrier'.[170] But in an unfamiliar place he is equally able to apply his generic spatial knowledge for deductive purposes – for example, using his familiarity with the conventional structure of cities to deduce the location of an auto-parts store: 'Which in any city is always right there on the same strip as the tyre stores and the auto dealers and the lube shops. Which in any city is always a wide new strip near a highway cloverleaf. Cities are all different, but they're also all the same.'[171]

Although Reacher's spatial understanding seems intuitive – or rather, tacit knowledge resulting from years of wandering – he often takes advantage of cartographic tools. In *The Midnight Line*, looking for a way to approach a back-country property and suspecting a set-up, Reacher visits a university geography department to gather intelligence: 'Reacher had

---

[168] Child, *The Midnight Line*, p. 175.
[169] Howell, 'Jack Reacher's carbon footprint', 35.
[170] L. Child, *Gone Tomorrow*. (Transworld Digital, 2009), p. 286, p. 289.
[171] L. Child, *One Shot*. (Transworld Digital, 2009), p. 148.

been at West Point when reading paper maps was still taught as a serious lifesaving skill. Terrain was important to an army. Understanding it was the difference between winning and getting wiped out.'[172] Consulting 'a hard-bound Wyoming topographical atlas about the size of a sidewalk paving slab',[173] he uses the information gleaned to approach the property surreptitiously. Later in the novel, he returns to the university to again consult the 'giant book of maps',[174] one of many times in the series when Reacher relies heavily on hard-copy maps.[175]

But Reacher's reading is not only cartographical. He is someone familiar with books – you might almost say that Reacher is 'bookish' in the loose sense with which this adjective is increasingly used to market novels and describe the people who buy and read them. Reacher holds people who read in high esteem. Talking to a man whose wife 'reads books', Reacher says, 'Tell your wife to keep on reading ... She sounds like a very smart woman.'[176] Conversely, non-readers are the subject of his mockery. When the drug-dealer villain of *The Midnight Line* replies to Reacher's question about whether he has 'read a book' by mentioning a title about the moon landing, the avenger replies facetiously, 'That's called non-fiction', before informing him that 'There's another kind, called fiction. You make stuff up, perhaps to illuminate a greater central truth.'[177] Elsewhere we learn that Reacher prefers fiction over non-fiction because the former is more honest in its lack of veracity.[178]

Reacher's reading, like his travelling, is haphazard: 'Battered paperbacks mostly, all curled and furry, found in waiting rooms or on buses, or on the porches of out-of-the-way motels, read and enjoyed and left somewhere else for the next guy.'[179] Reacher's love of second-hand fiction suggests that he is likely a default reader of bestsellers. However, his taste also seems to run to highbrow works. In *Blue Moon*, he holds his own in an intelligent conversation with his arts-graduate love interest: '[H]e read books when he could ... so he was able to keep up. A couple of times they found they had

---

[172] Ibid., p. 108. [173] Ibid. [174] Ibid., p. 107, p. 189.
[175] See also, for example: *Past Tense* and *No Plan B*.
[176] Child, *The Midnight Line*, pp. 43–4. [177] Ibid., p. 77.
[178] Child, *Make Me*. (Transworld Digital, 2015), p. 303. [179] Ibid.

read the same stuff.'[180] Occasionally he drops casual, ironic references to high literature: 'The man was listed as Steven Eliot, one l like the old poet. April is the cruellest month. That was for damn sure.'[181] Reacher has a penchant for etymology[182] and is a stickler for punctuation.[183] In *The Hard Way* (2006), he remembers being 'scandalized' as a child by the lack of punctuation in 'DONT WALK' signs: 'Ten thousand missing apostrophes in every city in America. It had been a secret thrill, to know better.'[184] In *No Plan B* (2022), he is 'annoyed' by a sign saying a door is 'alarmed', because 'an inanimate object couldn't feel trepidation'.[185] The whole plot of *Without Fail* (2002) hinges on a hyphen.[186]

While Reacher may be a book reader, his habit of picking up found paperbacks means that he is not much of a book buyer. In *The Hard Way*, set partly in the UK, he does make a couple of purchases from a big Oxford Street bookstore, although one is an ordnance-survey map and the other an atlas.[187] As this example suggests, his brief forays into bookshops are largely to gather intelligence, or else to kill time while waiting to gather intelligence. On these occasions, his impressions of new-book retail spaces are not overly positive. In *Make Me*, Reacher and his companions visit a bookshop in Menlo Park, California, to occupy themselves while waiting for a meeting in a nearby bar. He considers it 'a cool place, in every way, from its refrigerated temperatures to its customers'[188] – and for a man self-confessedly drawn to warm locations, this is certainly a negative. In *Gone Tomorrow*, set in New York City, Reacher needs information on a politician running for

---

[180] L. Child, *Blue Moon*. (Transworld Digital, 2019), p. 101.

[181] Child, *Persuader*. (Transworld Digital, 2015), pp. 40–41. Reacher similarly likens a situation to 'something out of Shakespeare' in *Make Me*, p. 302, and references Oscar Wilde in *No Plan B*, p. 234.

[182] See: Child, *The Midnight Line*, p. 64; Child, *The Affair*, p. 255.

[183] In this, as in many things, Reacher reflects the preoccupations of his creator. In *The Hero*, a non-fiction book, Child describes his conversations with his linguist daughter as well as the 'perils' of his own 'classical education'. L. Child, *The Hero*. (TLS Books, 2019), p. 12.

[184] Child, *The Hard Way*. (Transworld Digital, 2015), p. 94.

[185] Child and Child, *No Plan B*, p. 252.   [186] Child, *Without Fail*, pp. 265–66.

[187] Child, *The Hard Way*, p. 269.   [188] Child, *Make Me*, p. 303.

election. Rejecting the idea of an internet café due to his lack of aptitude with technology, he makes his way to a 'huge bookstore', walking straight past the tables at the entrance 'piled high with new titles' to reach the political biographies with their 'shiny jackets and glossy airbrushed photographs'.[189] The books found here are the opposite to the worn, dog-eared, abandoned copies that Reacher prefers. And this bookstore, too, is overcooled, its air-conditioning blasting Reacher as he sits at a third-floor window reading titles of interest. 'I used to feel bad about reading stuff in stores, with no intention to buy', he reflects, 'But the stores themselves seem happy enough about it . . . A new business model, apparently . . . the whole place looked like a refugee centre. There were people everywhere, sitting or sprawled on the floor, surrounded by piles of merchandise much bigger than mine.'[190] This is far from the restorative experience that, according to Audrey Laing and Jo Royle, characterises the chain bookshop, suggesting rather disconnection and languor. For Reacher, new bookshops are cold, clinical, and impersonal places for passive, disoriented consumers.

Ironically, then, Reacher would avoid those outlets – the overcooled megastores – that sell Reacher novels in the largest numbers and would be happier in a place like Quixotic Books or Black Swan, which do not even stock Reacher titles but encourage browsing and serendipitous finds, titles 'you might stumble across'.[191] What then would Reacher make of online bookselling, with its algorithms and targeted marketing?

3.5 Resisting Algorithms

In June 2022, *The Bookseller* declared Jack Reacher the 'bestselling book series of all time on Amazon.co.uk'.[192] About ten years earlier, Amazon had announced Child as the fifth author whose books surpassed one million sales on Kindle.[193] Reacher clearly does well in the context of online book retailers

---

[189]   Child, *Gone Tomorrow*, p. 68.   [190] Ibid.

[191]   Okenyo (Black Swan Bookshop), personal interview.

[192]   Bayley, 'Jack Reacher beats Harry Potter.'

[193]   'Lee Child and Suzanne Collins surpass one million Kindle books sold', *Business Wire* (6 June 2011), www.businesswire.com/news/home/20110606005670/en/ Lee-Child-and-Suzanne-Collins-Surpass-One-Million-Kindle-Books-Sold.

and the ebook market. Child was reportedly 'delighted to have hit [the million sales on Kindle] milestone',[194] but elsewhere has described his own reading practices in very different terms: 'When I was a kid, of course there was no Internet or structure for recommendations, none of these algorithm [sic] that if you like this you'll like that. Every discovery was to some extent random. And I try to replicate that whenever possible … I will choose books randomly based on how they look.'[195] Reacher's resistance to algorithms is even more pronounced than his creator's: as noted earlier, he doesn't even choose books but picks up 'battered paperbacks' where he finds them.

The existence of ebooks would presumably be news to Reacher, who is often amusingly oblivious to technological developments. 'I'm not great with phones', he admits, 'And I'm really not great with computers.'[196] In *The Hard Way*, Reacher wonders how a man who cannot talk communicates by phone and learns of a phenomenon called 'text messaging'.[197] Reacher's ignorance of computers and phones means that his occasional attempts to navigate the digital environment have an anthropological, defamiliarised air, as when he enters a hotel business centre in *Gone Tomorrow* looking for information online: 'I checked the screen icons and couldn't make much sense of them. But I found that if I held the mouse pointer over them, as if hesitating or ruminating, then a label popped up next to them. I identified the Internet Explorer application that way and clicked on it twice.'[198] Reacher is sometimes sceptical of the automatic superiority of the digital over the analogue, always preferring the hard copy where spatial orientation is required:

> 'I want to look at a map', Reacher said.
> 'Use your phone, man.'
> 'I don't have a phone.'

[194] Ibid.

[195] B. Robinson, 'Thriller writer Lee Child's inside scoop about his billion-dollar brand: Jack Reacher', *Forbes* (27 September 2019), www.forbes.com/sites/bryanrobinson/2019/09/27/thriller-writer-lee-childs-inside-scoop-about-his-billion-dollar-brand-jack-reacher/.

[196] Child, *Blue Moon*, p. 175. [197] Child, *The Hard Way*, p. 144.

[198] Child, *Gone Tomorrow*, p. 148.

'Really?'
'And I want to see detail.'
'Use satellite view.'
'All I would see is trees. Plus like I told you, I don't have a phone.'
'Really?'
'Where's the geography department?'[199]

This indifference is not hostility – indeed, two plots (*Make Me* and *The Sentinel*) centre on cybercrime, and Reacher is happy enough to engage with technology when required, often calling database specialists from his MP past to track down a suspect, and blithely commandeering other people's phones when necessary. But, like Sherlock Holmes, who knows the intricate details of various obscure poisons but is famously unaware that the Earth revolves around the Sun, Reacher is a 'need-to-know person where technology is concerned' and does not consider the online environment relevant to his personal existence.[200]

This determination to be off-grid is not only a choice for Reacher, but also a necessity if he is to remain anonymous and 'untraceable'.[201] In Mitchell's analysis, Reacher's resistance to the internet and other communication technologies is key to 'the anxiety informing all of Child's novels: that others know, and therefore control, too much about us'.[202] By avoiding the digital world, Mitchell explains, Reacher also remains undetectable within its systems, and hence immune to its attempts (through customer profiling, algorithmic marketing, cookies, etc.) to systematise his choices: 'That anxiety at being on the grid, accessible to anyone who might take the trouble to google him, represents a recent, more general cultural uncertainty about the possible costs of internet convenience.'[203] Mitchell relates this technophobia to Reacher's role within the narrative: '[I]t might be said that Reacher's desire to remain free of others' gaze, invisible as a subject, unknown to all but himself, finally represents a desire to remain outside of plot entirely.' At the end of each

---

[199] Child, *The Midnight Line*, p. 107.
[200] Child, *Make Me*, p. 167; A. C. Doyle, *A Study in Scarlet* (Penguin, 1981), p. 14.
[201] L. Child, *Bad Luck and Trouble*. (Transworld Digital, 2008), p. 13.
[202] Mitchell, 'Fairy tales and thrillers', 286. [203] Ibid., 286, 288.

book, Mitchell notes, Reacher departs for a destination unknown, 'disappear-[ing] as a figure about whom we can even speculate'. And yet just as Reacher uses the systems he avoids to track others down, so his seeming desire to escape his own plot 'necessarily contradicts the narrative impulse to tell his story and make him of interest'.[204] For Mitchell, who is interested in the contradictions that he sees as inherent to the 'appeal of formula narratives', this tension is key to what draws readers to Reacher.[205]

Broadening out Mitchell's argument beyond the text, we can identify a further contradiction between Reacher's preference for randomness – for battered paperbacks left at bus stops rather than stacks of new books in overcooled superstores – and the systematic processes that make the series a bestseller. Reacher titles are, of course, exactly the kind of books that make up these large stacks. The booksellers we interviewed often returned to the same word – 'reliability' – to describe the series' role in their stores. And a large part of this reliability is Child's predictable output of novels – one every October, in time for Christmas. While Reacher's appeal might draw on his love of 'crazy zigzags' and 'side trips', the series creates a predictable reading and retail experience. Reacher, then, resists the kind of systematic production and algorithmic selling that sent the series to an all-time top slot on Amazon UK. Thumb out, back to the viewer, and silhouetted against a road that disappears in the middle of a book's cover, Reacher – series and character both – promises a temporary escape from the predictable, linear routes which readers pass through to purchase and consume his stories.

In our introduction, we argued that Henry's *Book Lovers* romanticises material bookshops – their warmth, cosiness, familiar smells – in a way that belies the nature of the novel's own social-media-driven success. The Reacher series makes a related but converse move, dismissing the bestseller stacks at the front of superstores as well as the online environment with its controlling algorithms in favour of battered second-hand, accidentally acquired paperbacks. Both Child's and Henry's bestsellers, then, seem determined in their narrative content to contest the spatial logics and

---

[204] Ibid., 288. [205] Ibid., 278.

practices that produce and perpetuate their status in the fiction industry. Thus, while in focusing on Reacher we have chosen a series and genre that is especially productive to read in terms of space, place, and mobility, the approach we have developed can be applied productively to bestselling novels in quite different genres.

4 The Spatiality of the Bestseller

For the owner of Black Swan Bookshop, Alexander Okenyo, bestsellers function in 'two different directions': from the centre to the margin, and from the margin to the centre. The importance of the first direction, he told us, is 'getting international work here [New Norfolk, Tasmania], which is the function of any cultural organisation on the periphery'. As a commercial and cultural category, 'bestseller' works to bring books to the margins; they are a reliable indicator that local literary culture is globally connected. The second direction, which Okenyo values the most highly, is away from the margins: 'I'd say the main role of bestsellers is establishing Tasmanian and Australian presence.' For Okenyo, international bestsellers with 'whole publishing teams behind them' move through the publishing circuit with relative ease. 'Those books', he said, 'tend to sell themselves.' If a book has achieved the high visibility that comes with the nomenclature of the bestseller, Okenyo might keep one in store and a 'stack out the back'. When a customer requests such a title, he will 'just grab them a copy and they're on their way'. To raise the presence and profile of local authors and titles, by contrast, he generates buzz through store organisation, handselling, and the astute use of Instagram. The layout and organisation of Black Swan presents anyone entering the store with the promise that they 'might stumble across something'. When Okenyo wishes to translate this serendipitous experience into sales, he simply turns a book face out: 'Essentially, those face-out areas are my things that I want to sell because face out, one hundred percent, any book shop will tell you that you can sell that.'[206] These are also the titles that feature on the store's Instagram, about which

[206] Tim Jarvis of Fullers, where Okenyo once worked, concurred: 'Books that are selling very well will typically also be face out on the shelves where they live.'

he comments 'I almost don't think this store would work without social media.' At the heart of this bookshop and its ethos of curation and browsing is the connection Okenyo recognises and fosters between the books he sells and the people who buy them: '[T]he character of the bookshop is defined by the buyers, and the buyers in a good bookshop have personalities that . . . express themselves by the stock on the shelves.' The presence or absence of bestsellers is as much about our collective and individual identities as book buyers and readers as it is about logistics and commercial success.

Our conversations with Okenyo and the other booksellers we talked to highlighted for us three prevailing spatial ideas about novels that coalesce with special intensity in the category of the bestseller: *discoverability*, or the relative visibility and availability of books for sale; *portability*, or the relative ease and speed with which books move between locations and actors in the book market; and *relatability*, or the relative frequency and intensity with which books elicit social or emotional responses.

As 'high-profile products that drive publishing as an industry and connect it to other media sectors',[207] bestsellers are so widely available that they might seem to eschew the pleasures of new discovery. Several of the other booksellers we interviewed echoed Okenyo's view of bestsellers as the books that 'sell themselves' – the books, that is, for which high discoverability is taken for granted. Durkin explains, 'As booksellers, we don't necessarily need to handsell bestsellers because they do that themselves.' Wools-Cobb makes a related point when he refers to bestsellers as the books with 'the most exposure', or as literature's equivalent to 'fast fashion'. From this perspective, 'bestsellers' functions as a banner in the book industry that, as Danielle Fuller and DeNel Rehberg Sedo point out, 'reminds readers that books are commodities'.[208] They contend that 'Most readers recognize "bestsellers" as a category created by book industry professionals to draw attention to particular books.'[209] In other words, the classification works to move books into shopping bags, whether they are

---

[207] Driscoll and Squires, *The Frankfurt Book Fair*, p. 6.

[208] D. Fuller and D. Rehberg Sedo, *Reading Bestsellers and the Multimodal Reader*. (Cambridge University Press, 2023), p. 3.

[209] Ibid.

bookish tote bags or ⌂ icons on a mobile device. Bestsellers are highly visible *and* highly portable; they are found everywhere and – indeed, because – they travel easily from place to place, person to person. Bestsellers have 'of course, always sold across borders',[210] as Pascale Casanova states – a fact captured in the term 'airport fiction' – but the impact of globalisation and digitisation on today's fiction industry has dramatically enhanced their portability. Bestsellers are the driving edge of the digital revolution in publishing that defines the era Mark McGurl calls 'the age of Amazon', with e-commerce and self-publishing transforming where and how books are sold.

Bestsellers are also, as Driscoll and Rehberg Sedo argue, 'books that elicit responses: purchases obviously, but also discussion, debate and commentary'.[211] The portability of bestsellers connects here to the ubiquitous promise of their relatability, a promise that finds realisation in their reception. For literary author Charlotte Wood, '"Relatability" is a word that elicits a groan from those of us who see ourselves as sophisticated readers',[212] but it captures perfectly the specific promise of the bestseller that *you* will relate to a story because so many others have before you. The situated events of selling, purchasing, or reading a 'bestseller' are always multiplied across space and time, radiating outwards (as in an infinity mirror) from the individual encounter with a specific title to the myriad other encounters that make it a bestseller.

This section draws together the elements of our argument that the bestseller is a fundamentally spatial category, uniting in a heightened way the overlapping industrial, social, and textual dimensions of twenty-first-century book culture. We describe and analyse this zone of overlap by examining three devices that guide readers towards (and sometimes away from) bestsellers: bestseller lists; straplines that tout authors or books as 'bestsellers'; and 'shelf talkers' in bricks-and-mortar bookshops.

These three devices align roughly with the three concepts of discoverability, portability, and relatability. Bestseller lists, such as those published by the *New York Times* in the US or the *Sunday Times* in the UK, have long been

---

[210] P. Casanova, *The World Republic of Letters*. (Harvard University Press, 2004), p. 171.

[211] Driscoll and Rehberg Sedo, 'The transnational reception of bestselling books', 246.

[212] C. Wood, 'Reading isn't Shopping'.

the go-to reference to demonstrate the high discoverability of bestsellers.[213] Straplines such as 'Australia's Bestselling Author of Rural Fiction', 'The *Sunday Times* Bestselling Peter Grant Series', and 'The International Number One Bestseller'[214] signal the range of a title's movement. Handwritten shelf talkers recommending bestselling novels frequently emphasise relatability, directly addressing potential readers with a micro-story of personal connection. For example, one shelf talker at Fullers Bookshop shares a staff member's surprise at being genuinely moved by Ali Hazelwood's *New York Times* bestselling romance novel *The Love Hypothesis* (first self-published as a Star Wars fan fiction): 'Given all of the hype about this book, I was apprehensive to read it, but it is as wonderful as they say' (Figure 12).

These three devices do not exhaust the established and emerging marketing practices for moving bestsellers. Our argument would only gain strength if we turned our attention to other devices that promote bestsellers, such as book trade listicles, author endorsements in cover matter, or reader-voted awards. Myriad devices are behind the success of *The Love Hypothesis*, a telling example that demonstrates the marketing muscle, distributive power, and interpellative force of the 'bestseller'. A *Medium.com* listicle 'Your Fall 2021 Book Horoscope' identifies *The Love Hypothesis* (then a forthcoming release) as the 'perfect book' for Cancers.[215] The promise of a reading experience that is both generic and unique – for everyone and for *you* – is echoed in the endorsement from '*New York Times* bestselling author Christina Lauren' on the novel's front cover: 'Contemporary romance's unicorn; the elusive marriage of deeply brainy and delightfully escapist'.[216] The success of the publisher's campaign for this title is affirmed and amplified by the activities of readers online that sell

[213] See Wilkins and Bennett, *Writing Bestsellers*, p. 7.

[214] R. Treasure, *Cleanskin Cowgirls*. (HarperCollins, 2015), front cover; B. Aaronovitch, *Rivers of London*. (Gollancz, 2011), front cover; S. Meyer, *Twilight*, Special ed. (Atom, 2008), front cover.

[215] K. Barrett, 'Your fall 2021 book horoscope', *Medium.com* (29 August 2021), https://medium.com/from-the-library/your-fall-2021-book-horoscope-dfdaecd20b1c.

[216] A. Hazelwood, *The Love Hypothesis*. (Jove, 2021).

Figure 12 'The Global Bestseller and TikTok Sensation' *Love on the Brain* is displayed face-out in the new romance section at Fullers bookstore, alongside *The Love Hypothesis*.

even more copies. *The Love Hypothesis* came second in the 2021 Goodreads Choice Awards for Best Romance, behind Emily Henry's *People We Meet on Vacation*, with the covers of the top twenty titles illustrating publishers' faith in the vocabulary and imagery of travel to sell books by bestselling romance authors.[217] All these devices and more merit closer scrutiny, but in what follows we limit our attention to bestseller lists, cover straplines,

[217] 'Goodreads Choice Awards 2021: Best Romance', *Goodreads*, 2021, www.good reads.com/choiceawards/best-romance-books-2021.

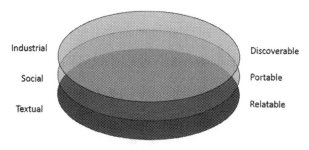

Figure 13 The Bestseller Biscuit.

shelf talkers, trusting that our approach lays the groundwork for future research.

As a starting point for our work in this section, we adapted the 'genre-worlds macaron' referenced in our introduction. The 'bestseller biscuit' (Figure 13) encapsulates our conceptual and methodological model, which builds on the genre-worlds approach. The processes and activities of the industrial layer make bestsellers more discoverable than other books; the middle social layer generates and maintains the greater portability inherent in bestsellers; and the textual layer reveals the prevalence of the idea and experience of relatability in the culture and industry of bestsellers. The three layers are always visible in and through each other.

4.1 'All of a sudden, pow': Bestseller Lists and Everywhere-ness

Bestseller lists are densely spatial in their form and operations. Rankings are determined by the volume of sales. Simply put, the book ranked #1 on a specific list has sold the most units according to the relevant source of data and context. Bestseller lists are key to the spatial logics and practices that drive book cultures and markets. Whether found at nytimes.com or in the window of a local bookstore, bestseller lists also function to communicate and uphold geographies of book publishing and distribution. They connect local, regional, national, and international markets for books at the same time as they reinforce boundaries between these geographical scales and contexts. 'Books', as Driscoll and Rehberg Sedo remark, 'are disseminated by an industry that is global, but not frictionless.'[218] Bestseller lists are conceived as ladders up (and down) which titles might climb, sometimes predictably for brand-name authors and sometimes so unexpectedly that they can 'trigger shifts in book culture and the publishing industry'.[219] It is beyond the scope (or purpose) of this Element to provide historical or economic analysis of the phenomenon of bestseller lists; others have done that work deeply and their research informs our thinking.[220] Our focus instead is to consider the role of bestseller lists in the industrial/discoverable layer of the bestseller biscuit.

We are in thorough agreement with Driscoll and Rehberg Sedo's statement that 'bestsellers are important focal points for *all* participants in book culture'.[221] In other words, bestsellers seem to be everywhere, with our research for this Element suggesting strongly that this sense of everywhere-ness is intensifying for professionals in the book industry, a finding that chimes with Giles Clark and Angus Phillips's conclusion that 'bestsellers are selling in larger quantities than ever'.[222] As we discuss in Section 3, for some of the booksellers we spoke to, the sense of everywhere-ness manifests more or less positively, with the omnipresence of bestsellers translating into reliable sales and return customers. For others, bestsellers just take up too much space to allow other types of books to flourish; they are a homogenising force in book culture. For Okenyo, 'The fear is you'll get less and less diversity in publishing, and less and less promotion of things that aren't particular things somebody in a boardroom knows will sell.' Wools-Cobb's business model for Quixotic Books seeks a route to sustainability that bypasses bestsellers. He told us, 'Something can be essentially called a bestseller before it even is sold.' 'Bestseller', in his

[218] Driscoll and Rehberg Sedo, 'The transnational reception of bestselling books', 244.
[219] Ibid., 246.
[220] See Wilkins and Bennett, *Writing Bestsellers*, for an excellent literature review about the meaning and significance of bestseller lists, historically, culturally, and economically, pp. 5–11.
[221] Emphasis added. Ibid., p. 246.
[222] G. Clark and A. Phillips, *Inside Book Publishing*, 6th ed. (Routledge, 2020), p. 120.

view, 'has almost become a genre of writing. It is a form of commerce rather than any indication of a book's merit.' Quixotic Books is therefore entirely uninterested in bestseller lists, appealing to customers with a particular sensibility and taste. Wools-Cobb explains:

> A lot of my business is designed around the concept of game theory . . . [Typically,] to do well, you need to sell the item that is going to sell the most – have the most foot traffic, the most exposure – where, game theory would suggest if you just don't do that because everyone else is doing that, you essentially hoover up all the other customers that are the minority, but are looking for something that's not what everyone else is doing.

Even here, however, in a small bookstore that neither pays attention to bestseller lists to select stock nor generates an in-store list, the significance of 'bestsellers' is palpable in their considered exclusion.

Murray's consideration of the verb 'selling' in relation to literature is pertinent to our argument that bestseller lists exemplify the industrial operations that determine a book's relative discoverability. She points to the word's 'double meaning': 'both the fundamental fact of the commercial transaction that is the bedrock of the book trade, as well as the more diffuse, colloquial sense of "selling"'.[223] Murray finds this 'double meaning' activated in the unprecedented and unrivalled commercial and cultural influence of online book retail. She writes, 'In perhaps the digital literary sphere's most dramatic imperializing gesture, book retailer websites, principally industry behemoth Amazon, have attempted to dominate all phases of books' lives, across all media.'[224] Visit any bestseller list online and you are one click away from buying a listed book on Amazon, with the retailer's own bestseller list ('Our most popular products based on sales. Updated frequently.') now one of the most prominent ranking engines for books. But

[223] S. Murray, *The Digital Literary Sphere: Reading, Writing and Selling Books in the Internet Era.* (Johns Hopkins University Press, 2018), p. 54.

[224] Ibid., p. 15.

the double meaning Murray describes is also in play when bestseller lists are generated for local – even hyper-local – markets.

We asked all the booksellers we interviewed whether there are categories that sell especially well in their store. Chris Vitagliano of Not Just Books talked about crime fiction and historical fiction, naming Child and Patterson as customer favourites. The store window of Not Just Books features a large screen that alternates digital posters for new releases with two store-generated bestseller lists – 'Bestsellers Adult' and 'Bestsellers YA & Children'. Vitagliano told us that these lists rank the top ten titles for each category by sale in the store: 'I look at our stats and I see what's selling.' When we visited in the first week of September 2022, the top seven of the ten titles on the Not Just Books 'Bestsellers Adult' list were novels. Numbers one to four were international bestsellers – Delia Owens's coming-of-age murder mystery *Where the Crawdads Sing*, Karin Slaughter's crime thriller *Girl, Forgotten*, James Patterson and David Ellis's serial killer thriller *Escape*, and Jill Hornby's historical romance *Godmersham Park*. The first Australian title on the list came in fifth – rural crime fiction *Stone Town* by Margaret Hickey. In sixth spot was *The Angry Women's Choir* by Tasmanian writer Meg Bignell, and in the seventh *Glow*, an adult fantasy novel by Californian Raven Kennedy.

The presence of *The Angry Women's Choir* and *Glow* on the shopfront bestseller list of this store illustrates two opposing points of distinction that Vitagliano identified about the place and function of 'bestsellers' in her bookshop in northern Tasmania: local flavour, and the power of social media marketing. Like all the booksellers we interviewed – except for Wools-Cobb of Quixotic Books – Vitagliano identified Tasmanian authors as central to her business. She speculated that Bignell's sales have been especially high in her store because the author, who lives four hours away on Tasmania's east coast, has visited the store, signing books and meeting customers. 'Tasmanians are proud', Vitagliano said, 'When they see that, "Oh, this is one of us," they want to get that book.' Durkin of Petrarch's said much the same thing: 'What we read, what we know, what we love, what we like to share with our community, is a Tasmanian bestseller.' The hyper-local pull of a novel like *The Angry Women's Choir* – by a Tasmanian and set in the state's capital city – stands in contrast to the global reach of the books that are bringing people to Not Just Books via social media.

The dual dependence on local and global bestsellers that Vitagliano identified was a thread throughout our interviews, with one pole represented by Tasmanian authors (frequently referred to by their first names) and the other by American-based TikTok bestsellers. *Glow*, the fourth book in Kennedy's Plated Prisoner series, is a prime example of the latter. Initially self-published, the series is now marketed by Penguin Random House as the 'TikTok sensation that's sold over half a million copies'.[225] Vitagliano elaborated on the significance of TikTok to her store's bestseller lists by sharing the impact of Colleen Hoover titles on her business. Hoover's internet-driven rise to the top of international bestseller lists exemplifies the global reach of 'BookTok' buzz: 'At the moment, we're seeing a massive rise in BookToks ... The Colleen Hoovers that've been out since 2016 and no one's really cared, but now she's on TikTok and social media, and all of a sudden, pow.'[226] When we visited Not Just Books, a carousel stacked with Hoover titles stood adjacent to a set of four shelves beneath a chalk-drawn sign, 'HOT #Booktok', with publisher-issued 'As seen on BookTok' shelf talkers reinforcing the message. We had similar conversations with other booksellers. Tim Jarvis shared that Fullers has been selling a lot of Hoover titles, which they 'wouldn't have a few years ago' and linked this new demand to BookTok. Tim Gott of Devonport Books described the BookTok effect as 'extraordinary', with the 'vast majority' of sales coming from a new adult market, and Durkin at Petrarch's pointed out the store's new 'BookTok' display (Figure 14).

The book industry has changed so dramatically in recent decades that there is now a scholarly consensus that the present era of book history can be described as one of 'revolution'. The impact of this revolution is felt

---

[225] 'The Plated Prisoner', *Penguin Random House*. www.penguin.com.au/series/the-plated-prisoner.

[226] Hoover's first self-published novel, *Slammed*, was published as an ebook in February 2012 with print editions appearing later that year. It is unsurprising that a remote brick-and-mortar bookseller dates their arrival as print products to several years later.

Figure 14 'We're seeing a massive rise in BookToks'. #BookTok displays at Not Just Books (left) and Petrarch's Bookshop (right).

even at the geographical outposts of the industry through phenomena such as BookTok bestsellers. John B. Thompson, in *Book Wars: The Digital Revolution in Publishing*, summarises this consensus: 'During the last few decades we have been living through a technological revolution that is as radical and far-reaching as any that came before in the long history of the human species.'[227] McGurl offers a name for this new era in his book, *Everything and Less: Fiction in the Age of Amazon*: '[T]he rise of Amazon is the most significant novelty in recent literary history, representing an attempt to reforge contemporary literary life as an adjunct to online retail.'[228] Murray uses the more capacious moniker of the 'internet era' in her *The Digital Literary Sphere: Reading, Writing, and Selling Books in the Internet Era*, while echoing McGurl in her references to the 'Amazon world'.[229] To borrow a metaphor from Murray, today it can seem that all roads in the literary sphere lead to Amazon.com.

---

[227] Thompson, *Book Wars*, p. vi.

[228] M. McGurl, *Everything and Less: Fiction in the Age of Amazon*. (Verso, 2021), p. xii.

[229] Murray, *The Digital Literary Sphere*, p. 54.

Unsurprisingly, when you click the 'BUY' button for a book on the *New York Times* bestseller list, the first retailer on the dropdown list is Amazon. Whatever we label the present era, bestseller lists persist as both a legacy of past eras and thrive as 'selling' devices (in both of Murray's senses) in our rapidly evolving culture of listicles and recommendation engines.

Like the booksellers we talked with, Driscoll and Squires acknowledge that the sense of 'pow' that accompanies bestselling authors and titles is generated through the collective work of many players in book culture: 'The buzz that surrounds a bestselling title can feel organic and mysterious. All of a sudden, a book seems to be "in the air", everywhere and nowhere. But the creation of book buzz takes concerted effort.'[230] One of the most visible artefacts of this concerted effort is bestseller lists, which work doubly to record and compare sales of individual titles in defined markets, and to drive future sales. As Fuller and Rehberg Sedo explain, 'Once the appellation of bestseller is made manifest in material form like a newspaper list, for example, it becomes a powerful paratext that can be used by authors, publishers, and booksellers in the marketing and selling of fiction.'[231] One way in which this appellation is used most often is through the straplines that grace the covers of countless novels, touting the text or its author as a bestseller.

4.2 'It is a voyage of discovery, and it is laid out for the browser': Straplines and Moving Bestsellers Somewhere

Straplines are standard marketing text printed on the covers of books that typically locate them in the industry in relation to the author's or title's previous success in commercial or critical terms. Within the bookstore, straplines that announce a book as a bestseller rely on the portability of the term across and within specific locations, acting to draw customers' attention amongst the myriad books on offer. For authors entering a bookstore, whether purposefully seeking a specific title or hoping to be surprised, such straplines enhance the navigability of the titles on offer.

---

[230] Driscoll and Squires, *The Frankfurt Book Fair*, p. 12.
[231] Fuller and Rehberg Sedo, *Reading Bestsellers*, p. 3.

As discussed in Section 3, for many of the respondents to our questions about buying books in TTP survey, the pleasure of book shopping is in 'browsing'. Their responses suggest an association between the idea and practice of browsing and positive localism, which manifests in a preference for independent bookstores over DDSs or online retailers. Many of the respondents who indicated that they buy most of their novels in 'physical bookstores in Tasmania' wrote of browsing, with remarkable similarity across these responses. Some described browsing as 'enjoyable in and of itself' and 'as fun as reading the book', with others drawing a line of connection between browsing, 'supporting local business' and 'discovering new books'. This association was echoed in our interviews with booksellers, who explained their investment in promoting and supporting the activity of browsing. Responses of TTP and our interviews evoke a specific retail ideal of happy browsing in a favourite bookstore, including the potential of 'chatting with the people who work there'. The serendipity of finding and buying a book on the shelves of a friendly bookstore might seem antithetical to the idea of bestsellers, an idea captured by a Tasmania Project respondent who wrote, 'I love browsing in bookshops and being surprised by what I find there.' The reality, however, is that bestsellers are powerfully advantaged by the marketing and retail conventions that sell books, with browsing more of a prepackaged tour than an adventure without a guide. Book covers with a strapline touting the author or title as a bestseller (henceforth 'bestseller straplines') function as especially effective signposts on this tour.

Squires argues that the marketing of books 'functions by endorsement, inclusion, and implication'.[232] Each of these three functions is powerfully at work in straplines such as '#1 *New York Times* bestselling author', 'The multi-million copy bestseller', or 'The thrilling sequel to the number one global bestselling phenomenon *The Fourth Wing*'.[233] Bestseller straplines seek

---

[232] Squires, *Marketing Literature*, p. 122.

[233] There are many examples of the strapline '#1 *New York Times* bestselling author', but we chose ours from Ann Cleeves's 2023 detective novel, *The Raging Storm*. 'The multi-million copy bestseller' is proclaimed on the cover of the fourth book in Richard Osman's Thursday Murder Book Club series, *The Last Devil to Die*, clearly referring to the series rather than this 2023 novel. 'The

to move books by creating consumer confidence with a message of mass endorsement, by activating consumer desire for inclusion in the cultural mainstream, and by fuelling consumer loyalty with the implication that an author's next book will be as good as their previous work. In her analysis of the marketing functions of the covers of Booker-Prize-winning novels, Squires analyses straplines as 'part of the marketing mix' that leads to a book's 'commodification' and 'physically places it in the marketplace'.[234] She argues that a strapline 'sends out signals to a potential readership', acknowledging that '[h]ow those signals are received is open to the normal interference of marketing communications: for some, the strapline may be an attraction to buy and read the book, but for others . . . it may be a warning to avoid'.[235] We follow Squires in our interpretation of bestseller straplines, with the caveat that the label 'Bestseller' issues a different (but not utterly opposed) invitation to readers as 'Booker Prize Winner', a distinction that Squires points to with her analysis of the literary 'consecration' mobilised by the latter.[236] Our focus is on how the signals issued by bestseller straplines are so readily transported across spatial boundaries.

Bestseller straplines manifest the social algorithms of book marketing. They act as sorting devices to carry particular authors and titles to book buyers in dispersed locations. The promise of consumer satisfaction issued by the algorithmic function of bestseller straplines – on covers and centre-screen on a book's Amazon page – is 'a prime piece of marketing'[237] that generates and perpetuates the idea of bestselling novels as supremely portable. That bestsellers reach everywhere means they must be reliably present in every

thrilling sequel to the number one global bestselling phenomenon *The Fourth Wing*' is *Iron Flame*, book 2 in Rebecca Yarros's Empyrean series, available for purchase on pre-order at the time of writing.

[234] C. Squires, 'Book marketing and the Booker Prize' in N. Moody and N. Matthews (eds.), *Judging a Book by Its Cover: Fans, Publishers, Designers, and the Marketing of Fiction*. (Routledge,2016), p. 71, p. 75.

[235] Ibid., p. 81. [236] Ibid., p. 75.

[237] Ibid., p. 75. We have adapted this phrase from Squires, who uses it to explain the consecrating force of Booker straplines: 'The judgement delivered by the prize panel and heralded on the cover is a prime piece of marketing, and plays a role in defining cultural value that should not be underestimated.'

'somewhere', a spatial logic that inheres in the strapline as a signpost for booksellers and book buyers alike.

Bestseller straplines were highly visible in every bookstore in our sample, even in the two that consciously oriented their business away from the bestseller. For example, in Black Swan, while there was not a Reacher in sight, face-out displays included titles with the standard straplines: Emily St. John Mandel's *Sea of Tranquility* – from the '*New York Times* Bestselling Author of *Station Eleven*'; John MacGregor's *Lean Fall Stand* – from the 'Bestselling Author of *Reservoir 13*'; and 'International Bestselling Author' Miriam Toews's *Fight Night* (Figure 15). Bestseller straplines were plentiful in Quixotic Books, with the store's remainder business model meaning that these were not on new releases but on older titles, such as Australian Jane Harper's 2016 debut crime fiction *The Dry*, Tim Johnston's 2015 '*New York Times* Bestseller' *Descent*, and Agnès Martin Lugand's 'International Bestseller' *Happy People Read and Drink Coffee* (Figure 15). Bestseller straplines position books by orienting potential readers in local space and time, in constant relation to regional, national, and international geographies of the fiction industry. They do not undermine the narrative of book shopping 'as a voyage of discovery', but rather make bestsellers dominant landmarks on that voyage, whether travellers choose to go ashore or not.

Straplines exemplify the publishing industry's concerted effort to lead readers towards and into bestsellers. Jonathan Gray, in his study of paratextuality in film and television, writes, 'Paratexts are the greeters, gatekeepers, and cheerleaders for and of the media, filters through which we must pass on our way to "the text itself," but some will only greet certain audiences.'[238] As we have seen in other examples of bestsellers discussed in this Element, the strapline is only one aspect of the paratextual delivery of these books, always working together with other components. Child may not have chosen his hero's name – Reacher – to signal his ambitions to reach every corner of the world book market, but 'The World's Number One Bestseller' and 'The New Jack Reacher

[238] J. Gray, *Show Sold Separately: Promos, Spoilers, and Other Media Paratext.* (New York University Press, 2010), p. 17.

Figure 15 Selling bestsellers face-out at Black Swan Bookshop (left) and Quixotic Books (right).

Thriller' certainly work together.[239] Similarly, all of Emily Henry's titles and cover designs play on the positive association of bestsellers with leisure and relaxation to communicate that the books everyone reads can deliver special and memorable experiences for readers. In conjunction with these other paratextual devices, straplines reinforce the status of bestsellers as the most discoverable and portable product of the fiction industry, whether people choose to sell, buy, or read them or not.

4.3 'You Will Not Put This Book Down': Shelf Talkers and Locating Bestsellers Here

For booksellers, shelf talkers are cards with short recommendations or reviews by members of staff that are affixed to shelves to promote specific books.[240] The term also refers to printed cards produced by bookstore chains or publishers to promote titles, authors, or themed campaigns (e.g.,

---

[239] L. Child, *The Secret*. (Bantam, 2023).

[240] 'Shelf talkers' are also commonly used in public libraries and schools, including staff- and client- or student-produced cards to promote engagement with books. See T. Cattanach and S. La Marca, 'Shelftalkers: Empowering student voice',

'Hot Read'; '#10 BEST SELLER'; '3 + 1 FREE').[241] For retailers more broadly, 'shelf talkers' – less commonly called 'shelf barkers' and 'shelf shouters' – refers variously to small cards with handwritten text taped to shelves; to printed tickets or stickers provided by manufacturers; or to the clips or plastic sleeves designed to hold printed cards. Writing for *The Guardian*, Peter Robins remarks on the visibility of shelf talkers in bookshops: 'You have almost certainly seen a shelf-talker, even if you didn't know it was called that: one of those little cards attached to the shelf on which a bookshop – or, better, an individual bookseller – pours out their enthusiasm for the title above.'[242] A contributor to the American Booksellers Association blog describes the shelf talker as a '5 1/8" X 2 3/8" workhorse',[243] implying both its increasing standardisation as a format and genre of book marketing and its reliability in moving books off the shelves. As text-based '[p]oint of purchase stimuli',[244] bookshop shelf talkers are a distinctive and valued marketing device that has attracted virtually no scholarly attention. They are, however, an ideal focus for understanding the habits of thinking and behaviour that bring physical books into the immediate reach of potential buyers and readers. In relation to bestsellers, shelf talkers are point-of-sale paratexts that help sustain a productive tension for publishers and booksellers between the social and intimate spatialities of the bestseller, delivering the books that reach everywhere to a specific 'here'.

Synergy, 19 (2021), www.slav.vic.edu.au/index.php/Synergy/article/view/527/520.

[241] Such shelf talkers are ubiquitous, but our sources for the three listed here were Hudson News at Ronald Reagan Washington National Airport and W. H. Smith at Changi International Airport, Singapore.

[242] P. Robins, 'Do you listen to bookshop shelf talkers?' *The Guardian* (19 May 2009), www.theguardian.com/books/booksblog/2009/may/19/2.

[243] '50 words or fewer: The art of writing shelf talkers', *American Booksellers Association* (7 April 2010), www.bookweb.org/news/50-words-or-fewer-art-writing-shelf-talkers.

[244] M. Wedel and R. Pieters, 'Introduction to Visual Marketing' in M. Wedel and R. Pieters (eds.), *Visual Marketing: From Attention to Action*. (Lawrence Erlbaum Associates, 2008). p. 1.

The practice of 'showrooming' means, however, that the conversion of shelf-talker engagement into a sale may not happen in-store or be of a physical book. Clark and Phillips define showrooming simply as 'the use of smartphones in store to check comparative prices',[245] linking the practice to the impact of online retailers, especially Amazon, and ebooks. Added to the *Oxford English Dictionary* in March 2017 and modified in July 2023, the word emerged in the first decade of the twenty-first century in the US, with the first usage identified by the *OED* being a tweet from 2009: 'Back from a loooooong day of showrooming.'[246] The OED entry indicates that the term now has broad application for all types of retail: 'The action of going to a showroom or showrooms to view goods or merchandise; spec. the practice of visiting a shop or shops in order to examine a product before buying it online at a lower price.'[247] Showrooming, however, has special resonance for the book trade, with the second recorded usage in the OED etymology coming from *Publishers Weekly* in December 2011: 'If "showrooming" wasn't part of the industry lexicon before last week, it is now, thanks to Amazon's price check app.'[248] Steven E. Jones remarks on the potential of QR codes to 'make it even easier and less obvious to engage with what book retailers bitterly call "showrooming", using the bricks-and-mortar store to shop for what they buy online'.[249] In this context, shelf talkers (for which the *OED* has no entry as yet) can be read as direct appeals from booksellers to book buyers to browse *and buy* in store, to act 'here' and in person rather than to defer

---

[245] Clark and Phillips, *Inside Book Publishing*, p. 18. See also E. Bowker and C. Somerville, 'Sun treasure: Can the traditional public library service survive in contemporary Britain?' in A. Baverstock, R. Bradford and M. Gonzalez (eds.), *Contemporary Publishing and the Culture of Books.* (Routledge, 2020), p. 89: '"showrooming": the opportunity to view titles [customers] were thinking of buying, before ordering online'.

[246] 'showrooming, n.' *Oxford English Dictionary*, July 2023, https://doi.org/10.1093/OED/4960733938.

[247] Ibid. [248] Ibid.

[249] S. E. Jones. *The Emergence of the Digital Humanities*. (Routledge, 2014), p. 44.

to the digital literary sphere. They evoke a sense personal relationship between bookseller and book buyer, and between reader and book.

Paradoxically, the proliferation of handwritten shelf-talkers – analogue equivalents of the micro-memoirism that thrives online – may be as much a product of the Age of Amazon as Goodreads reviews or Patreon-funded series. In the face of digital disruption to book retail, they appeal to choose customers' locality and community over expedience and price point. At the same time, they echo and offer similar pleasures to the countless numbers of snappy readers' reviews online. They mark bookstores as, to quote Jones, places 'where the doubleness of digital and physical is breaking down'.[250] This doubleness manifests spatially in the intersecting phenomena of show-rooming and shelf talking.

In Launceston's Petrarch's Bookshop, where the shelves are positively a-flutter with handwritten recommendation cards, shelf talkers are affectionately called 'shelfies' (a nickname that gestures to online bookish social media tools that play on the conventions of the 'selfie'[251]). Owner-manager Andy Durkin drew a connection between the store's heavy use of shelf talkers and the books that sell the most copies in the store: 'We focus on not only what we read, but what we read is what we sell . . . We employ specifically readers, and we employ readers that can talk to people . . . What our staff read is often also our bestseller.' All members of staff in Petrarch's, she said, 'will regularly pop a shelfie onto what they've read – what they've loved – and give a brief overview of what they've enjoyed about it.' Tim Jarvis at Fullers concurred, sharing that 'shelf talkers do increase the movement of the stock for those titles' and can 'take something that's not selling at all and turn it into something that turns over regularly'. 'When they really work', he said, 'they can create a bestseller.' Many of the shelf talkers in

[250] Jones, *The Emergence of the Digital Humanities*, p. 39.

[251] See L. Fletcher, J. McAlister, K. Temple and Kathleen Williams. '#loveyour-shelfie: Mills & Boon Books and How to Find Them/ #loveyourshelfie: Mills & Boon books et comment les trouver', *Mémoires du livre/Studies in Book Culture*, 11 (2019), www.erudit.org/en/journals/memoires/2019-v11-n1-memoires05099/1066945ar/.

Devonport Bookshop are personally penned by Tim Gott, including special cards for 'Tim's Book of the Week ... As reviewed on [local radio station] 7AD'. Durkin's, Jarvis's, and Gott's confidence in the efficacy of shelf talkers echoes the view of US bookseller Joe Drabyak: 'Word-for-word a well-crafted shelf talker can be the most effective means of recommending a book to an avid reader.'[252] They are, in these terms, a surrogate for direct handselling, passing a book from one avid reader to another.

The appeal of shelf talkers for booksellers and book buyers alike connects to the distinctive spatial phenomenology of browsing in a bookshop, which contributes to their social function as affinity spaces at once contained and multiply connected as networked environments. Cynthia Compton gushes about the sense of affinity that shelf talkers create on the *Publishers Weekly* blog: 'Those charmingly bookish handwritten cards, sometimes covered in fancy plastic protectors, sometimes laminated, and often just taped to the edge of the bookshelf are like little peeks into the soul of a store.'[253] For Robins, shelf talkers help book buyers relate to the communal atmosphere of a bookstore, inspiring 'a sense of connection with the people who created the nice space I'm currently in – the rest of the shop serves as a character reference'.[254] When shelf talkers recommend or reference bestsellers, they zoom in from the global marketplace to the utterly local, from the generalised or mass reader implied by a bestseller strapline to the individual directly or indirectly addressed by a handwritten note about one bookseller's reading experience – from everywhere to here.

Shelf talkers are devices that seek to inspire relatability for people considering the purchase of a book in a specific store. The main purpose

---

[252] J. Drabyak quoted in '50 words or fewer'.

[253] C. Compton, 'Show us your shelftalkers', *Shelf Talker – Publishers Weekly* (10 February 2020), http://blogs.publishersweekly.com/blogs/shelftalker/?p=32392.

[254] Robins, 'Do you listen to bookshop shelf talkers?'

of a shelf talker is to move stock off shelves with a pithy review that makes a customer carry a book from shelf to counter and out of the store. They generate customer loyalty to bookstores, promote local authors, and provide read-alike information to assist readers with book selection. Shelf talkers offer snapshot analyses of books that locate books industrially ('Award-winning journalist Trent Dalton is a new player in the world of contemporary Australian fiction'), socially ('Fans of *The Rosie Project*, Liane Moriarty, Marian Keyes, and our own Esther Campion will love this novel'), and textually ('Arnott's great trick is to describe a masculine world with a lyrical precision that allows access to the protagonist's unexpressed emotions').[255] Shelf talkers personalise and localise the promise that a bestseller makes to potential customers that, as one penned by Tim Gott reassured customers browsing in Devonport Bookshop, 'You will not put this book down.'

Spatial ideas are intrinsic to the ways bestselling novels are marketed, distributed, sold, and read. In this Element, we have examined how bestsellers exist within and travel between different types of retail spaces, from the local to the global, virtually and physically. Through paratextual, textual, and site-based analysis, we have demonstrated the centrality of geography to the commercial promise of these books. We have argued that bestsellers are engines designed to move books and to move people: to shift stock to and from the shelves of bookshops and to provoke reactions in their readers. And while the category functions on a global scale, crediting titles with an appeal that reaches from metropolitan centres to the ends of the Earth, bestsellers can also be highly local, when the term is deployed by individual bookshops to celebrate books that appeal specifically to their immediate community. We have shown how the term signifies

---

[255] Shelf talkers for: *Boy Swallows Universe*, by Trent Dalton at Petrarch's Bookshop; *Star Crossed* by Minnie Darke at Devonport Bookshop; and *Limberlost*, by Robbie Arnott at Fullers Bookshop.

in industrial, social, and textual contexts and the impossibility of disentangling these components of its meaning. Elements are slim volumes and bestsellers are big books, but we hope that our multi-layered analysis offers new inroads for understanding the relationship between space, place, and popular fiction.

Bibliography

#enterbabel. *TikTok Creative Centre*, https://ads.tiktok.com/business/crea tivecenter/hashtag/enterbabel/pc/en?countryCode=AU&period=7.

Aaronovitch, B. (2011). *Rivers of London*. London: Gollancz.

About. *Devonport Bookshop*, www.devonportbookshop.com.au/pages/ 4693-ABOUT.

About. *Dymocks Books and Gifts*, www.dymocks.com.au/about.

About Fullers Bookshop. *Fullers Bookshop*, www.fullersbookshop.com.au/.

About QBD. *QBD*, www.qbd.com.au/site/about/.

About Us. *Not Just Books*, https://notjustbooks.com.au/pages/about-us.

About Us. *Petrarch's Bookshop*, www.petrarchs.com.au/about-us.

Alter, A. (2013). Sci-fi's underground hit. *The Wall Street Journal*, 14 March, www.wsj.com/articles/SB100014241278873246786045783407520 88305668.

Babel. (2023). *Title Key*, 29 September, https://e.hc.com/book/97800630 21440.

Barber, R. (2017). Lee Child: The man who's sold 100 million books. *Stuff*, 5 April, www.stuff.co.nz/entertainment/books/91106765/lee-child-the-man-whos-sold-100-million-books.

Barrett, K. (2021). Your Fall 2021 Book Horoscope. *Medium.com*, 29 August, https://medium.com/from-the-library/your-fall-2021-book-horo scope-dfdaecd20b1c.

Bathurst, R. & Crystall, A. (2019). Attending *Night School:* Leadership lessons at the Jack Reacher academy. *Journal of Management and Organization*, 25(3), 430–44.

Baverstock, A., Bradford, R., & Gonzalez, M., eds. (2020). *Contemporary Publishing and the Culture of Books*. London: Routledge.

Bayley, S. (2022). Jack Reacher beats Harry Potter as Amazon reveals bestselling book series. *The Bookseller*, 23 June, www.thebookseller

.com/news/jack-reacher-beats-harry-potter-as-amazon-reveals-best selling-book-series.

Blakesley, E. (2014). Lee Child's pure, uncomplicated hero. In G. Hoppenstand, ed., *Critical Insights: The American Thriller*. Ipswich: Salem Press, pp. 88–98.

Borsuk, A. (2018). *The Book*. Cambridge, MA: The MIT Press.

Bowker, E. & Somerville, C. (2020). Sun treasure: Can the traditional public library service survive in contemporary Britain? In A. Baverstock, R. Bradford and M. Gonzalez, eds., *Contemporary Publishing and the Culture of Books*. London: Routledge, pp. 77–95.

Brown, S., ed. (2006). *Consuming Books: The Marketing and Consumption of Literature*. Abingdon: Routledge.

Browse. *Oxford English Dictionary*, www-oed-com.ezproxy.utas.edu.au/ view/Entry/23882.

Browser. *Oxford English Dictionary*, www-oed-com.ezproxy.utas.edu.au/ view/Entry/23883.

Carlick, S. (2022). Emily Jenry and Erin Morgenstern: How TikTok changed authors' careers. *Penguin*, 9 August, www.penguin.co.uk/ articles/2022/08/emily-henry-and-erin-morgenstern-how-tiktok- changed-our-careers.

Carter, D. (2016). Beyond the Antipodes: Australian popular fiction in transnational networks. In K. Gelder, ed., *New Directions in Popular Fiction: Genre, Distribution, Reproduction*. London: Palgrave Macmillan, pp. 349–70.

Casanova, P. (2004). *The World Republic of Letters*. Cambridge, MA: Harvard University Press.

Cattanach, T. & La Marca, S. (2021). Shelftalkers: Empowering student voice, *Synergy*, 19(2), 1–7, www.slav.vic.edu.au/index.php/Synergy/article/ view/527/520.

Chalke, B. (2022). The Hobart Bookshop, personal interview with Elizabeth Leane (8 September).

Child, L. (2010). *61 Hours*. London: Bantam.

    (2013). *A Wanted Man*, Bantam.

    (2008). *Bad Luck and Trouble*, Transworld Digital.

    (2019). *Blue Moon*, Transworld Digital.

    (2008). *Die Trying*, Transworld Digital.

    (2011). *Echo Burning*, Bantam.

    (2008). *Echo Burning*, Transworld Digital.

    (2009). *Gone Tomorrow*, Transworld Digital.

    (2019). *The Hero*, TLS Books.

    (2015). *Make Me*, Transworld Digital.

    (2008). *Nothing to Lose*, Transworld Digital.

    (2009). *One Shot*, Transworld Digital.

    (2019). *Past Tense*, Bantam.

    (2014). *Personal*, Transworld Digital.

    (2008). *Persuader*, Transworld Digital.

    (2011). *The Affair*, Transworld Digital.

    (2005). *The Enemy*, Bantam.

    (2009). *The Enemy*, Transworld Digital.

    (2008). *The Hard Way*, Transworld Digital.

    (2009). *The Killing Floor*, Transworld Digital.

    (2017). *The Midnight Line*, Transworld Digital.

    (2023). *The Secret*, Bantam.

    (2008). *The Visitor*, Transworld Digital.

    (2008). *Tripwire*, Transworld Digital.

    (2008). *Without Fail*, Transworld Digital.

    (2010). *Worth Dying For*, Bantam.

    (2010). *Worth Dying For*, Transworld Digital.

Child, L., & Child, A. (2021). *Better Off Dead*. Transworld Digital.

(2022). *No Plan B.* Transworld Digital.

Clark, G. & Phillips, A. (2020). *Inside Book Publishing*, 6th ed. London: Routledge.

Compton, C. (2020). Show us your shelf talkers. *Shelf Talker – Publishers Weekly*, 10 February, http://blogs.publishersweekly.com/blogs/ shelftalker/?p=32392.

Crane, R. & Fletcher, L. (2017). The proximity of islands: Dirk Pitt's insular adventures. In R. Crane and L. Fletcher, eds., *Island Genres, Genre Islands: Conceptualisation and Representation in Popular Fiction.* London: Rowman & Littlefield International, pp. 71–84.

D'Alessandro, A. (2022). 'Dungeon Crawler Carl' author Matt Dinniman inks with WME. *Deadline*, 26 October, https://deadline.com/2022/ 10/dungeon-crawler-carl-author-matt-dinniman-wme-1235155412/.

Dietz, L. (2015). Who are you calling an author? Changing definitions of career legitimacy for novelists in the digital era. In G. Davidson and N. Evans, eds., *Literary Careers in the Modern Era.* London: Palgrave Macmillan, pp. 196–214.

Donohue, K. (2013). Underground hit puts sci-fi in a new light. *The Washington Post*, 12 March, p. C1.

Doyle, A. C. (1981). *A Study in Scarlet.* London: Penguin.

Driscoll, B. (2019). The rise of the microgenre. *The University of Melbourne: Pursuit*, 13 May, https://pursuit.unimelb.edu.au/articles/the-rise-of-the-microgenre.

Driscoll, B. & Rehberg Sedo, D. (2020). The transnational reception of bestselling books between Canada and Australia. *Global Media and Communication*, 16(2), 243–58.

Driscoll, B. & Squires, C. (2020). *The Frankfurt Book Fair and Bestseller Business.* Cambridge: Cambridge University Press.

Drivers of Tasmania's Future Population Health Needs. (2020). *Department of Health (Tasmania)*, www.health.tas.gov.au/sites/default/files/

2022-06/Drivers%20of%20Tasmania%27s%20Future%20Population
%20Health%20Needs_0.pdf.

50 words or fewer: The art of writing shelf talkers. (2010). *American Booksellers Association*, 7 April, www.bookweb.org/news/50-words-or-fewer-art-writing-shelf-talkers.

Durkin, A. (2022). Petrarch's Bookshop, personal interview with Lisa Fletcher (5 September).

Fletcher, L., McAlister, J., Temple, K., & Williams, K. (2019). #love-yourshelfie: Mills & Boon books and how to find them/ #loveyour-shelfie: Mills & Boon books et comment les trouver. *Mémoires du livre/Studies in Book Culture*, 11(1), 1–33, www.erudit.org/en/jour nals/memoires/2019-v11-n1-memoires05099/1066945ar/.

Frost, S. (2017). Readers and retail literature: Findings from a UK public high street survey of purchasers' expectations from books. *Logos*, 28(2), 27–43.

Fuller, D. (2004). *Writing the Everyday: Women's Textual Communities in Atlantic Canada*. Montreal: McGill-Queen's University Press.

Fuller, D. & Rehberg Sedo, D. (2023). *Reading Bestsellers and the Multimodal Reader*. Cambridge: Cambridge University Press.

Gee, J. P. (2005). Semiotic social spaces and affinity spaces. In D. Barton and K. Tusting, eds., *Beyond Communities of Practice: Language, Power and Social Context*. Cambridge: Cambridge University Press, pp. 225–29.

Gelder, K. (2004). *Popular Fiction: The Logics and Practices of a Literary Field*. London: Routledge.

Glover, D. & McCracken, S. (2012). Introduction. In Glover and McCracken, eds., *The Cambridge Companion to Popular Fiction*. Cambridge: Cambridge University Press, pp. 1–14.

Gott, T. (2022). Devonport Bookshop, personal interview with Lisa Fletcher (8 September).

Grey, J. (2010). *Show Sold Separately: Promos, Spoilers, and Other Media Paratexts*. New York: New York University Press.

Gregoriou, C. (2007). *Deviance in Contemporary Crime Fiction*. London: Palgrave Macmillan.

Hayot, E. (2021). Video games and the novel. *Daedalus*, 150, 178-187.

Hazelwood, A. (2021). *The Love Hypothesis*. New York: Jove.

Henry, E. (2022). *Book Lovers*. Dublin: Penguin Books.

Hermes, J. (2000). Of irritation, texts and men: Feminist audience studies and cultural citizenship. *International Journal of Cultural Studies*, 3(3), 351–367.

Howell, P. (2022). Jack Reacher's carbon footprint: Reading airport novels irresponsibly. *Literary Geographies*, 8(1), 19–44.

Humanities showcase: Celebrating a string of successes. (2022). *University of Tasmania: News and Stories*, www.utas.edu.au/?a=1593645.

Jack Reacher author Lee Child passes writing baton to brother. (2020). *BBC News*, 18 January, www.bbc.com/news/entertainment-arts-51162838.

Jack Reacher Series. *Penguin Random House*, www.penguinrandomhouse.com/series/JAC/jack-reacher/.

Jack Reacher: UK. *Penguin Random House*, www.jackreacher.com/uk/.

Jack Reacher: US. *Penguin Random House*, www.jackreacher.com/us/.

Jansen, A. M. Y. (2021). The most bookish cities in the world. *Book Riot*, 2 July, https://bookriot.com/bookish-cities/.

Jarvis, T. (2022). Fullers Bookshop, personal interview with Elizabeth Leane (17 November).

Jones, S. E. (2014). *The Emergence of the Digital Humanities*. London: Routledge.

Katsoulis, M. (2013). Literary preview of 2013. *The Telegraph*, 2 January, www.telegraph.co.uk/culture/books/9756380/Literary-preview-of-2013.html.

Kenlin. r/JackReacher. *Reddit*, www.reddit.com/r/JackReacher/com ments/8av1le/mule_crossing_wy/.

Kuang, R. F. (2022). *Babel or the Necessity of Violence: An Arcane History of the Oxford Translators' Revolution*. London: HarperVoyager.

Kuang, R. F. (2023). *Amazon Australia*, 29 September, www.amazon.com .au/R-F-Kuang/e/B0788VXRHP/ref=aufs_dp_mata_dsk.

Laing, A. & Royle, J. (2013). Examining chain bookstores in the context of 'third place'. *International Journal of Retail & Distribution Management*, 41(1), 27–44.

Latimer, E. (2021). Home and home-less: Narrating and negating the domestic in contemporary crime fiction series. *Clues*, 39(1), 72–85.

Lee Child and Suzanne Collins surpass one million Kindle books sold. (2011). *Business Wire*, 6 June, www.businesswire.com/news/home/ 20110606005670/en/Lee-Child-and-Suzanne-Collins-Surpass-One-Million-Kindle-Books-Sold.

Li, J. (2010). Choosing the right battles: How independent bookshops in Sydney, Australia, compete with chains and online retailers. *Australian Geographer*, 41(2), 247–262.

Luyt, B. & Heok, A. (2015). David and Goliath: Tales of independent bookstores in Singapore. *Publishing Research Quarterly*, 31, 122–31.

Macquarie University and the Australia Council for the Arts. (2016). Reading the reader: A survey of Australian reading habits. *Australia Council*, https://australiacouncil.gov.au/advocacy-and-research/reading-the-reader/.

Magner, B. (2014). Shantaram: Portrait of an Australian bestseller. *Antipodes*, 28(1), 213–25.

Martin, A. (2015). *Reacher Said Nothing: Lee Child and the Making of Make Me*. New York: Bantam.

   (2019). *With Child: Lee Child and the Readers of Jack Reacher*. Cambridge, MA: Polity.

McGurl, M. (2021). *Everything and Less: Fiction in the Age of Amazon*. London: Verso.

Meyer, S. (2008). *Twilight*, Special ed. London: Atom.

Miller, L. J. (2007). *Reluctant Capitalists: Bookselling and the Culture of Consumption*. Chicago: University of Chicago Press.

Mitchell, L. (2009). Fairy tales and thrillers: The contradictions of formula narratives. *Literary Imagination*, 11(3), 278–90.

Moody, J. (2018). 100 million copies sold, a sale every NINE seconds and 61 weeks at No. 1: The remarkable stats behind the Jack Reacher series. *Mirror*, 3 April, www.mirror.co.uk/news/uk-news/100-million-copies-sale-every-12259882.

Murray, S. (2006). Publishing studies: Critically mapping research in search of a discipline. *Publishing Research Quarterly*, 22(4), 3–25.

 (2018). *The Digital Literary Sphere: Reading, Writing and Selling Books in the Internet Era*. Baltimore: Johns Hopkins University Press.

Muse, E. J. (2022). *Fantasies of the Bookstore*. Cambridge: Cambridge University Press.

Nanquette, L. (2017). The global circulation of an Iranian bestseller. *Interventions*, 19(1), 56–72.

National, state and territory population. (2024). *Department of Treasury and Finance Tasmania*, https://www.treasury.tas.gov.au/Documents/Population.pdf.

Noorda, R. & Marsden, S. (2019). Twenty-first century book studies: The state of the discipline. *Book History*, 22(1), 370–97.

O'Brien, G. M. T. (2017). Small and slow is beautiful: Well-being, 'socially connective retail' and the independent bookshop. *Social & Cultural Geography*, 18(4), 573–95.

Quixotic Books. *Quixotic Books*, www.quixoticbooks.com.au/.

Okenyo, A. (2022). Black Swan Bookshop, personal interview with Elizabeth Leane (21 October 2022).

Reserve listing. *Tasmania Parks and Wildlife Service*, https://parks.tas.gov
.au/about-us/managing-our-parks-and-reserves/reserve-listing.

Robinson, B. (2019). Thriller writer Lee Child's inside scoop about
his billion-dollar brand: Jack Reacher. *Forbes*, 27 September, www
.forbes.com/sites/bryanrobinson/2019/09/27/thriller-writer-lee-
childs-inside-scoop-about-his-billion-dollar-brand-jack-reacher/.

Salamanca's independent bookshop. *The Hobart Bookshop*, https://www
.hobartbookshop.com.au/page/about.

Semel, P. (2021). Exclusive interview: 'He Who Fights with Monsters:
Book Two' author Shirtaloon. 15 July, https://paulsemel.com/exclu
sive-interview-he-who-fights-with-monsters-book-two-author-shirta
loon/.

Shirtaloon: He Who Fights with Monsters - Chapter 1: Strange business.
Royal Road, www.royalroad.com/fiction/26294/he-who-fights-
with-monsters/chapter/386590/chapter-1-strange-business.

Patreon, www.patreon.com/Shirtaloon.

Showrooming. *Oxford English Dictionary*, www.oed.com/dictionary/show
rooming_n?tab=meaning_and_use#1197750040.

Snapshot of Tasmania: High level summary data for Tasmania in 2021. (2022).
Australian Bureau of Statistics, 28 June, www.abs.gov.au/articles/
snapshot-tas-2021.

So then there was a bookshop. *Quixotic Books*, www.quixoticbooks.com.au/
about.

Squires, C. (2007). *Marketing Literature: The Making of Contemporary
Literature in Britain*. Basingstoke: Palgrave Macmillan.

(2016). Book marketing and the Booker Prize. In N. Moody and
N. Matthews, eds., *Judging a Book by Its Cover: Fans, Publishers,
Designers, and the Marketing of Fiction*. Milton Park: Routledge,
pp. 71–82.

Steiner, A. (2017). Select, display, and sell: Curation practices in the
bookshop. *Logos*, 28(4), 18–31.

Tasmania's Top 10s of 2022. *Libraries Tasmania*, https://libraries.tas.gov
.au/news/top10sof2022/.

The home of web fiction. *Royal Road*, www.royalroad.com/welcome.

The Tasmania Project. *University of Tasmania: Community and Partners*.
www.utas.edu.au/community-and-partners/the-tasmania-project.

Thompson, J. B. (2021). *Book Wars: The Digital Revolution in Publishing*.
London: Polity.

Touma, R. (2022). Babel: The BookTok sensation that melds dark academia with a post-colonial critique. *The Guardian*, 8 September, www
.theguardian.com/books/2022/sep/08/babel-the-booktok-sensa
tion-that-melds-dark-academia-with-a-post-colonial-critique.

Trager Bohley, K. (2010). The bookstore war on Orchard Road: A study of
contemporary sponsors of literacy and ideologies of globalised book
retailing in Singapore. *Asian Journal of Communication*, 20(1), 104–123.

Treasure, R. (2015). *Cleanskin Cowgirls*. Sydney: HarperCollins.

Turan, K. (2009). The thrill is back (so is Reacher). *Los Angeles Times*, 19 May,
www.latimes.com/archives/la-xpm-2009-may-19-et-book19-story.html.

Vermeulen, J. (2017). The lonely road to freedom: Jack Reacher's interpretation of an American myth. *Clues: A Journal of Detection*, 35(1),
113–23.

Vitagliano, C. (2022). Not Just Books, personal interview with Lisa Fletcher
(6 September).

Watson, D. (2017). Derivative creativity: The financialization of the contemporary American novel. *European Journal of English Studies*, 21(1),
93–105.

Web browser. *Oxford English Dictionary*, www-oed-com.ezproxy.utas.edu
.au/view/Entry/226695.

Wedel, M. & Pieters, R. (2008). Introduction to visual marketing. In
M. Wedel and R. Pieters, eds., *Visual Marketing: From Attention to
Action*. New York: Lawrence Erlbaum Associates, pp. 1–8.

Wilkins, K., & Bennett, L. (2021). *Writing Bestsellers: Love, Money, and Creative Practice*. Cambridge: Cambridge University Press.

Wilkins, K., Driscoll, B., & Fletcher, L. (2022). *Genre Worlds: Popular Fiction and Twenty-First-Century Book Culture*. Amherst: University of Massachusetts Press.

Wood, C. (2018). Reading isn't shopping. *Sydney Review of Books*, 14 August, https://sydneyreviewofbooks.com/essay/reading-isnt-shopping/.

Wood, Z. (2023). Indie bookshop numbers hit 10-year high in 2022, defying brutal UK retail year. *The Guardian*, 6 January, www.theguardian.com/books/2023/jan/06/indie-bookshop-numbers-hit-10-year-high-in-2022-defying-brutal-uk-retail-year.

Wools-Cobb, T. (2022). Quixotic Books, personal interview with Lisa Fletcher (28 November).

Acknowledgements

This Element was made possible by the patient and enthusiastic support of our families. We want to thank our research assistants in the early stages of the project, Eliza Murphy and Kurt Temple. We want to acknowledge the excellent support of our colleagues at the University of Tasmania, especially Emmett Stinson for his thoughtful feedback on our ethics application, and Ami Seivwright for expert guidance with the Tasmania Project. We are especially grateful to Caylee Tierney for her diligence and her commitment to this project as our research assistant. This project was granted ethics approval by the University of Tasmania Human Research Ethics Committee (Project ID 27475).

Cambridge Elements ≡

Publishing and Book Culture

SERIES EDITOR
Samantha Rayner
University College London

Samantha Rayner is Professor of Publishing and Book Cultures
at UCL. She is also Director of UCL's Centre for Publishing,
co-Director of the Bloomsbury CHAPTER (Communication
History, Authorship, Publishing, Textual Editing and
Reading) and co-Chair of the Bookselling Research Network.

ASSOCIATE EDITOR
Leah Tether
University of Bristol

Leah Tether is Professor of Medieval Literature and Publishing
at the University of Bristol. With an academic background in
medieval French and English literature and a professional
background in trade publishing, Leah has combined her
expertise and developed an international research profile in
book and publishing history from manuscript to digital.

ABOUT THE SERIES

This series aims to fill the demand for easily accessible, quality texts available for teaching and research in the diverse and dynamic fields of Publishing and Book Culture. Rigorously researched and peer-reviewed Elements will be published under themes, or 'Gatherings'. These Elements should be the first check point for researchers or students working on that area of publishing and book trade history and practice: we hope that, situated so logically at Cambridge University Press, where academic publishing in the UK began, it will develop to create an unrivalled space where these histories and practices can be investigated and preserved.

Cambridge Elements $^{\equiv}$

Publishing and Book Culture

Bestsellers

Gathering Editor: Beth Driscoll

Beth Driscoll is Associate Professor in Publishing and
Communications at the University of Melbourne. She is the
author of *The New Literary Middlebrow* (Palgrave Macmillan,
2014), and her research interests include contemporary reading
and publishing, genre fiction and post-digital literary culture.

Gathering Editor: Lisa Fletcher

Lisa Fletcher is Professor of English at the University of
Tasmania. Her books include *Historical Romance Fiction:
Heterosexuality and Performativity* (Ashgate, 2008) and *Popular
Fiction and Spatiality: Reading Genre Settings* (Palgrave
Macmillan, 2016).

Gathering Editor: Kim Wilkins

Kim Wilkins is Professor of Writing and Deputy Associate
Dean (Research) at the University of Queensland. She is also
the author of more than thirty popular fiction novels.

Elements in the Gathering

The Hroswitha Club and the Impact of Women Book Collectors
Kate Ozment

Publishing Romance Fiction in the Philippines
Jodi McAlister, Claire Parnell and Andrea Anne Trinidad

Printed in the United States
by Baker & Taylor Publisher Services